PLANNING TO CRACK A NUT

PLANNING TO CRACK A NUT

TONY JENKINS

best wishes Ann

Tony Jenkins

July 19th 1996

Illustrations by Rowena Cass

CAEDMON OF WHITBY

By the same author: THE STORY UNFOLDS (1991)
                     AT A PRICE THAT'S VERY NICE (1992)

ISBN 0 905355 43 1

Published by: CAEDMON OF WHITBY, 128 Upgang Lane, Whitby.
Printed by: SMITH SETTLE, Ilkley Road, Otley.

Dedicated to the memory of my father, C.S. Jenkins
who made me what I am.

ACKNOWLEDGEMENTS

I have to thank many people but chiefly two builder friends of mine, Bill Jackson and Des Berridge, for without their tuition and skill the building and restoration of this small farm enterprise would not have been possible. And also Chris Hayes for helping me to lay the foundations and Rowena Cass for her inspired drawings.

Contents

I am a jolly ploughman. (Courtesy of Dennis Dobson.)

THE JOLLY PLOUGHMAN

I am a jolly ploughman
I plough the fields all day
A hasty thought came to my head
That I should change my ways.

So I parted with my horses
And laid aside my plough
And put away my hames and chains
I'll no longer need them now.

It was a scene of heartbreak
At the market place that day
I said goodbye to Prince and Grace
And slowly walked away.

And I bought myself a tractor
A little Stanford Ford
The engine sang out sweetly
At a price I could afford.

But I missed the sounds of nature
And the birds no longer sang
The tractor barked and spluttered
And the church bells never rang.

So I'm off to buy my horses back
To harness to the plough
I've never missed two friends so much
But I know I miss them now.

The lark was me that morning
And sunshine was the day,
With "C'mon old gal" and "Gee up Prince"
We were proudly on our way.

So come on you jolly ploughman
Who follow behind the plough
We'll say a prayer for yon old 'oss
And by gum we'll say it now.

FOREWORD

The much publicised planning dispute has been an item of discussion from the day it began and indeed, right up to the present time, and continues to be so.

In June 1989, without a shred of evidence that this small development had caused even the slightest traffic problem, or even any problems, in over four years, and without taking into consideration our efforts, ongoing concern and awareness of environmental protection, the National Park Planners wielded the big stick. 'The access was unsuitable, and the site inappropriate'. We were, they said 'detrimental to the environment!' They were going to close us down.

But the planning dispute went much deeper than that, and it cut much deeper. As a result of certain conditions subsequently imposed upon us by North Yorkshire County Council, we were to become embroiled in several more years of legal dispute.

A private summons which was later described as a 'cynical and pointless piece of litigation which nobody in his right mind would contemplate if he were paying his own costs' was taken out against us. The plaintiffs claim was supported by a Legal Aid Certificate.

Oh yes, we won on all counts, but should anybody be expected to fight so desperately to protect what can only be described as a small country living? It took almost five years to resolve and it cost us dearly.

Well thankfully it is now resolved, and although we found it very traumatic, I think it played a vital role in changing certain attitudes. There is now a much better understanding of the necessity for conciliatory discussion and realistic, on the spot advice.

INTRODUCTION

Behind this idyllic facade, and I am sure behind many others, there are a few skeletons in the cupboard and a few stories to tell.

This book includes the planning dispute. It also looks at the people involved and the parts they play. Onerous conditions imposed upon us led subsequently to another battle. This time in the civil court.

Behind every dispute there has to be motivation, sometimes high handed bureaucracy, sometimes jealousy and sometimes sheer bloody mindedness. It can be played singly but usually the players (shall we call them that?) come together and appear to become a conspiracy.

Someone is possibly pulling the strings of the puppets but this player is hard to identify. There are no rules.

In any game you have two main strategies. Attack and Defence. I think in any serious confrontation it would have to be the former. If you feel threatened to the extent of being wiped out you don't hesitate.

With apologies to Rudyard Kipling, I have got to say that there was no way that I was going to see the things I gave my life to broken, nor was I prepared to hear the truth I had spoken, twisted by knaves to make a trap for fools.

This is a unique story about Staintondale Shire Horse Farm, which has been described as both a concept and an ideal. You would defend that sort of situation with your last breath. Questions born of curiosity are still being asked. I hope this book at least answers some of them.

It is not about recrimination. It is about the truth and its success and satisfaction in the face of adversity.

The book starts with some of the background which is interesting and colourful and includes some wonderful facets of life here.

It describes some of the hard and painstaking effort that it took to create such a wonderful award winning enterprise. It is not about a small business development, it is about a lifetime's commitment to building a dream.

It has taken twenty-five years.

I have already written two very successful small books so to the readers of those I say 'Here is a third - enjoy it!'

Tony Jenkins
June 11th 1994

CHAPTER ONE
Going too far

To put this whole story in perspective we have to go back to the year 1975 and a year that took me to The Great Yorkshire Show with a yearling filly called Princess.

It had all started with the purchase of this young horse from a farm just outside a small town in Lancashire. A lovely and rewarding experience I shall never forget. It was Monday 28th April. I had made the journey to the farm with a Land Rover and trailer — just in case! As I remember the farm it was situated fairly high up in the Pennines and I imagine it could be pretty bleak in winter.

They were very nice people and I enjoyed their warm hospitality and Lancashire frankness. I suspected the lady of the house wasn't really too eager to see the horse go. She was obviously very attached to it.

We seemed to talk for hours but I don't remember much haggling about the price — a little bit of banter perhaps. Eventually we all shook hands and I was now the proud new owner.

We now had to persuade our yet unnamed yearling into my aged single axle Rice horse trailer. Fortunately she was used to being tied in a stall so with a few strategic moves and a bit of persuasion — food I think — in she went.

It was pouring with rain and as grey as slate. I was beginning to wish that we hadn't talked quite so long. The drive back to Scarborough was horrendous. It was lashing down as I made the M62 intersection and pulled on to the motorway. The wistful face of the lady at the farm still stuck in my mind — a touch of sadness.

By now I was in the thick of it. Rain pouring down, heavy spray from goods vehicles and a general feeling of claustrophobic gloom — it was like driving through a nightmare. It got darker, and suddenly I was numbed by my own thoughts — no trailer lights! Oh heck! — for want of a better adjective that's printable. I pressed

1

...and a bit of persuasion —
food I think!

harder on the accelerator but I knew I wasn't going to make it before lighting up time.

Suddenly a new and more pressing thought slowly dawned upon my mental horizon — The trailer — it had no glass in the frame of the small front window. Without hesitation I signalled and pulled on to the hard shoulder. This was an emergency.

I looked in through the frame and I could have cried. This young filly was saturated, all the driving rain and spray had been thrust towards the front of the trailer and had found its mark. She was wet and shivering. Quickly I rummaged in the back of the Land Rover and by a stroke of good fortune found a large piece of canvas sheet. I quickly rolled it up and stuffed it into the window frame. 'Hang on, beautiful' I said to the filly — 'I will soon have you home'.

This set-back spurred me on and I shrugged off the grey mantle — let's get back to Staintondale I said to myself. I decided to leave the motorway at Tadcaster and get across the A1 — bit quieter I thought — especially with my lights problem. What a journey — It seemed like crossing the Atlantic.

Once we got off the M62 I stopped and climbed into the trailer. The young horse was fine now and had warmed up. On we went crossing a few minor roads until we eventually joined the A64. Relief wasn't in it. I had been more concerned about my lovely newly purchased young filly than I was about producing my vehicle documents at the local Police Station.

Home at last. Our interesting stone flagged Souvenir Shop was at that time the cow byre and that was to be home for this special young lady at least for the night. I unloaded her down the ramp and led her into the middle standing.

A good rub down with a straw wisp and a feed of bran and corn and she would be as good as new.

I carried in a couple of bales of straw and made her a deep bed. An overstuffed hay net was my final offering, together with a full water bucket. It was a very tired young animal that eventually hit the sack that night, and that was only the horse.

The next morning I awoke with a feeling of sheer exuberance. What a wonderful find, I couldn't believe my good luck. I got dressed quickly and rushed out to the cow byre.

The filly greeted me with a sharp whinny as I stood proudly looking her over. 'You're lovely' I said 'I shall call you Princess.'

An overstuffed hay net was my final offering.

Late that day as promised I rang the previous owners. 'Yes we got home safely in spite of everything' and then, 'Yes she's fine and no problems.' Then came the next question. 'What are you going to call her?' 'Well', I said 'I am going to call her Princess because of her lovely nature and good looks.' There was a silence and then a wistful voice said 'I'm pleased — that's what I was going to call her!' . . .

As a comparative newcomer to Shire Horses and with even less experience of the show ring I decided Princess was worth showing off if nothing else.

At that time there was a Shire Breeder in Staintondale who was helped by his enthusiastic if sometimes outspoken Son in Law. I decided to take Princess round for an opinion.

'You've been amongst Showmen for that one' said the older man. 'Nice little filly' echoed his companion.

'Is thi goin to show 'er?'

Praise indeed and I knew it was frank and genuine.

'Tek' er ti Yorkshire' he answered his own question in a strong local dialect. 'I'll 'elp thi' and — she'll need a bit o schoolin an a set of bevils.'

Why not I thought — start at the top!

My new adviser, Victor, was as good as his word. He came round

Hang on, I'll get behind her with a whip.

and taught me the basics of showing technique.

He took up a judging position. 'Right now, walk her away from me in a straight line and then turn her inwards towards you and walk her back towards me. Make her walk on — tickle her with your whip!'

We did this a few times and then:-

'Not bad, keep her at it though and keep her head up. Now we are going to try the trotting out. This time make her trot and make her look lively and pick her feet up.'

It wasn't too good — 'Hang on. I'll get behind her with the whip — she's got to show herself better than that.' The response was amazing, she started to use her hocks and went really well. 'Keep that up every day for an hour or so and she'll soon get the hang of it, your job is to make sure she impresses the judges. You'll need a set o bevils.'

I looked puzzled 'Bevel shoes — she'll need to be shod,' he said 'Go and see Blacksmith at Cloughton.'

I was lucky, the village Blacksmith, Edgar, was a heavy horse enthusiast and although regretfully passed away now, in his years of smithying, had shod more than his share of cart horses. His eyes seemed to light up when I told him what I wanted. 'Young Shire 'oss eh?' He paused for thought 'Bring her down, let's have a look.'

I almost flew back to Staintondale, hooked the trailer on and back I went.

His wealth of knowledge was his stock in trade, he cast an admiring glance over Princess. 'Good Shire feet' he said 'Plenty of depth at the heel!' He continued 'Yorkshire Show eh? Well I know a man who will look her over for you. Hang on I'll ring and see if he's in.'

Such enthusiasm and goodwill really impressed me — what a friend to know.

Within minutes his 'man' appeared. A man who is still around as

4

I write this book and among many of the names I would like to mention. For reasons that will eventually take shape this book is for the most part 'No Names, no pack drill!

This man stood back to make his assessment. He moved forward and ran his hand slowly down the cannon bone to the coronet pressing down hard.

'Will she pick her feet up?' he enquired, at the same time proceeding to do just that. 'Not bad feet', he said 'She'll look better shod.' He stood back. 'Walk her round a bit.' His eyes explored every contour. 'Yes' he said 'She'll show all right and she's big enough.'

The Blacksmith spoke, 'Right bring her down on Thursday night about seven — it's oer warm in't day time at the moment for shoeing them things.'

I duly arrived at the forge and led the horse inside. Again I was to be impressed. There on the anvil was a set of perfectly made, hand forged bevel shoes — and without so much of a rough measurement being taken. This was the work of a master craftsman. To this day I still have two of those shoes.

My new adviser was now looking towards the great day, 'When you get to the Showground you will need somebody to plait her up and do her tail. I have a mate who works for Bernie Hopgrove — go and see him and tell him I sent you.'

Plaiting up and bobbing tails were a foreign language to me — it sounded very complicated. The Bernie Hopgrove is a fictitious name and on arrival at the Showground with my youngest daughter Anita it became even more so, because the man in question wasn't there and neither was his 'man'. My heart sank into my boots 'What on earth do we do?' This was the Great Yorkshire Show and not the village fete. But help was at hand.

A man sat outside one of the stables in the heavy horse section. He had watched our arrival on what was the eve of the first day of the show. I think having my young daughter with me helped, people seem to get into conversation easier. He called across. It was 'Hi there bonnie lad' and 'How are you pet' to Anita. I recognised the Geordie influence and the warmth and hospitality of his tone of voice. It turned out he was very much a Yorkshireman! However ...

We walked towards him. 'And what are you showing?' His enthusiastic chatter drew us towards him like a magnet. He was a

5

small dapper little man with twinkling eyes. I explained our predicament after telling him about our yearling filly Princess. He told us his name was Frankie Walker.

'No problem', he said 'I will come round to the box at 7 a.m. and plait her up and put you right. He smiled 'Is this young lassie showing her — she ought to be, Judges will tek to her!'

Late that evening we met two other very helpful men from my native Derbyshire and they immediately took to Anita. One of them later became a good friend and in spite of my Derbyshire origins insisted on calling me 'Ilkley Moor bah tat'. His name was Iain Yates.

It was a wonderful introduction and put my mind at ease. We were taken to the fodder yard, water supply and all the other areas we needed to know. A big showground can be a nightmare to newcomers and especially one who hasn't shown before.

The great day dawned and we were up long before sunrise. Our friend and guardian angel kept his word to the second. Not only did he plait Princess up but he also showed us how to show off the feather on her front feet.

'I'll walk down to the main ring with you when it's time.' It was all very re-assuring.

Now we were walking to our destiny. A number card hung around Princess's neck and she looked resplendent in her plait and flights.

I couldn't believe the overwhelming public interest in these heavy horse classes. It was nothing short of besotted adulation. We had a job even getting into the ring. 'If this support' I mused 'could be channelled into a business enterprise it would be a runaway success.' I was in business myself and very much aware of the values of public interest from a publicity point of view. 'Shire Horses are a magnet', I concluded.

It was a small class and we were up against the country's and county's top professionals. Princess by name, Princess by nature was a model of behaviour.

We were a well placed fourth and for a first attempt we were delighted. As I walked proudly out of the ring, Anita rushed towards me — 'She was super', she said, 'Ought to have won!'

A man suddenly appeared from nowhere, he leaned heavily against me almost losing his balance. I smiled, he had been enjoying his day. There was a distinctive aroma of malt liquor. His

6

Princess was a model of behaviour.

speech was slurred, 'Sheez not daft that filly', pause for concentration, 'Sheez not daft but sheez just gone too far!!'

It slowly dawned what he was trying to say. Princess had more than her share of white markings (I shall wisely leave it at that) 'But' he leaned speaking with some effort and occasionally losing his balance, 'I know a good Stallion that'll just suit her — ish mine!'

That Stallion turned out to be Carr Coming King, and the man's name? Well let's just say that although I didn't use his Stallion we became good friends and had a few sociable drinks together.

As I write this book, as many visitors will know, we still have Princess who is now 19 years old. She blessed us with our own Premium Stallion Mascot, which she foaled in 1980.

CHAPTER TWO
PIONEER OR ECCENTRIC ENTREPRENEUR

I had returned from the Yorkshire Show with some brand new thoughts. First and foremost I think was the rather poor prospects for breeding Shire horses. The oil scarcity problem seemed to have receded, people had accepted the higher prices that were originally going to bankrupt the Western World and more important, self sufficiency with horse power was becoming no more than a forlorn hope.

Oh yes, the showing species still did well from a price point of view but these accounted for a very small percentage. There is no such thing as an average price for a Shire Horse — call it what you will. It is either good or bad.

It seemed that private motoring will survive and that means tourism and visitors to the area.

By now I had got really hooked on Shire horses and I had been looking seriously at my inadequate buildings and stables. The yard was a mess. An assortment of scrappy implements from the horse era and nowhere to renovate them.

Slowly a plan began to emerge from the debris in my mind.

What about some nice new stalls — tailor made and purpose built for these big horses. Even our new yearling had had to stoop to get into our cow byre. And — my enthusiasm gathered pace — an adjoining building to restore and finally house all this equipment. And then the yard — still the original old muddy fold yard. What about concrete with a man made stone sett pattern?

I knew a man who could do it — it was me!

That same day I measured up the area in between the stone buildings and the hay barn (now Video Studio). I carefully drew up a plan and decided exactly what could be fitted into it.

By now I had a lovely mental picture — it is the scene our visitors see everyday. In this mental picture I saw people — all the

I knew a man who could do it — it was me!

faces I had seen at the Great Yorkshire Show. The same lovely faces, young and old alike. Faces filled with nostalgia and thoughts of happy days of youth. I saw faces filled with admiration and wonder. Small children standing back in amazement but each and every one in love with a Shire Horse. I saw fulfilment in my picture, and a great deal of pleasure to be shared. To do what I wanted to do was going to need capital and although I had a small business I was struggling financially and cash was at a premium.

Well nothing else for it, I shall have to go and sell my idea to a bank — they usually have money.

In 1975 it was not easy. The main question asked was 'can you service the loan?' This means — how much does your enterprise earn and can it afford to borrow? For a new enterprise needing funds for development it was a non-starter.

'Oh yes, quite a good idea Mr. Jenkins but .... Shire Horses as an attraction — well, er, you are obviously an enthusiast but, er, are there many like you?'

I thought I was an enthusiastic and confident talker on the subject. I oozed with nostalgia and buttercup meadows, granny's pegged rugs and mangles. They were not impressed. With my spirits flagging I had one final thrust. I telephoned for an appointment at a Yorkshire Bank — there, said it! The Manager's name was Mr. Flowers.

but . . . Shire Horses as an attraction?

10

He listened carefully and was very interested. "You have a unique idea there and I think the plan well thought out and a viable proposition. It may take you a while to get established but I am sure you will succeed. From this bank's point of view, to secure any sort of loan I would require satisfactory balance sheets of any previous business and of course the transfer of your account. Whether we manage finally to help you is of course up to you but I wish you well and I shall keep an eye out for your progress."

At that time my balance sheets wouldn't have impressed anybody and the thought of rushing into my own bank shouting "That's it! I shall transfer my overdraft elsewhere" (reminiscent of Tony Hancock) would have brought only one reaction — 'Good'.

It was now 1976 and things were beginning to look better. Whatever happened now I had made my mind up. I was going to do it and fund it myself over a period. At that time planning permission was not required for certain farm buildings and so from that point of view I could make a start.

What I was concerned about was spending a lot of money over a fairly long period and then having problems when I decided my enterprise was sufficiently developed to open to the public.

I wrote to the National Parks Officer to clarify the position. This was the reply dated 13th September 1976.

Dear Sir,

Shire Horse Centre and Farm Park Staintondale

I refer to your letter dated 2nd September 1976 and your site meeting with my assistant Mr. Elm in connection with the above proposal.

It would appear that in the first place you are to run the holding as an agricultural unit and as such no planning permission will be required.

I would suggest, therefore, that when you are in a position to discuss definite alterations to running of the unit, you contact my assistant Mr. Elm.

Yours faithfully,
National Park Officer

It was a reassuring letter or so I thought. Now with my plan in operation I would make a start.

First job was to clear the area. It was a ramshackle scene. Two old hen huts, a wooden turkey verandah and the remnants of a wood and corrugated iron building about on its last legs. I had been told it was the old Threshing shed and had originally housed a barn thresher which was fed by taking a couple of tin sheets from the roof. The machine was then fed from the top.

One lovely story from the 1930's. The farm man had gone to the house to get the men's wages for half a day's threshing. Miss Dawson came to the door 'Now William' she said 'how much for the men?' 'Well I'm afraid its three shillings each Miss Dawson.' (15p) 'Three shillings! Whatever is the world coming to!' Ah well, inflation and all that.

Once we had a clearance, levelling began and a lot of the stone used for building the dry stone wall on the yard was excavated from the foundations of the new building.

When the trenches were out, the strip concrete foundations were in and I began building. With my previous building experience and knowledge I was able to order a full load of Tilcon hollow building blocks. I specified an hydraulic off loader. Quality blocks, in quantity at the right price. That driver made history. In 1976 I think it was the largest vehicle to negotiate the lane and the bridge over the beck. He had to shunt to get round. Then there was the ten foot gate almost set in a pond — most times it was. It's hard to believe now, but for fifteen years we put up with a permanently blocked pond overflow that flooded the road in wintertime and made it impossible to go out without wellingtons. Things got even worse later on, but more of that later.

These drivers were always cheerful — 'your moat was a bit of a problem, there wasn't room to get past the vehicle without falling in it!' He had to shut the gate. 'It's not my moat' I said, 'Only wish it were, I could do something about it.' He meticulously unloaded the blocks all carefully stacked beside the footings. 'Well at least you got them here' I said and thrust a pound note in his hand. I won't bore you with the building work but it was the start of the making of a dream.

Once finished, new concrete floors were laid and the stables decorated. I choose original old fashioned shades of dark red and green.

Talk about Five Star accommodation — the horses were very suspicious at first. We even had to spread a bit of horse manure around.

I reckon this to be the biggest D.I.Y. self build kit ever, and that was only the start.

'Your moat was a bit of a problem.'

Now to clear the yard of some of the clutter. The most awkward of these rusting relics was a turn of the century McCormick self-tie binder in near scrap condition.

It just happened that my son Glenn was off work through injury after a motorcycle accident. He was, like me, really a mechanic by trade and useful with his hands. We dragged the machine into our new posh work area and looked it over. All the sheet metalwork was in tatters. After careful examination we decided a new bed (metal floor to platform) new guards and a new band box would have to be made.

The self-tie binders created havoc on their arrival, as thousands of farm workers engaged in scything and sickling saw them as a threat to jobs. They really were a revolution. The mechanical corn reaper had been bad enough but this was a threat to a gang of field workers. They were around for well over fifty years.

Anyway, back to work on the binder. Surprising though it may seem it didn't take too long. I think painting it was the worst job.

We really went to town, and an old friend of mine George Watson of Sneaton even made a brand new set of spindles for the reel.

We are more than fortunate still to have some of his generation around. When the last old fashioned farrier and wheelwright has passed on, rural communities will be a poorer place. They will be skills lost forever. The binder is now in its new quarters and the band box even has a supply of genuine oiled binder band! The binder pole is in the roof above and all it requires to drive it is a three horsepower team.

That is the story of one item out of many. We have a lot to do yet but we were on our way.

CHAPTER THREE
BLOWING UP THE WIND

A very funny incident happened in March 1976. It was the sale at Kirkbymoorside at 12 noon of the entire contents of a Blacksmiths Shop and Smithy. A sad event really, but not without a touch of romantic aura. These were the years of my future destiny, and collecting all the pieces of rural memorabilia I needed took me into some remarkable situations. They say every picture tells a story, well I have got to say that there is a story to practically every piece of yester-year that we have in our colourful collection. Putting and piecing it together and embarking on painstaking restoration work took me nine whole years. Life was pretty uneventful from a domestic point of view, our elderly neighbour who incidentally owned the pond, still kept a few cows but they were never a problem. In wintertime they were in and the gate the driver had the problem with, was left open. Back to the events of the day.

Quite a few of us had decided to attend the sale for various reasons — two of the local blacksmiths' sons and their apprentice were amongst the crowd and obviously a lot of local people and what we call curiosity seekers.

We had decided to go early and have a look round and then go for a pint at a local hostelry. Duncan the apprentice wanted a farrier's tool box and tools — there were several.

I wanted anything that was reasonably priced that would lend itself to my project. We had our few drinks and returning in excellent humour waited for the Auctioneer's bell to commence the sale. It started quietly as most auctions do, each waiting for another to start the bidding and then hopefully coming in on the act.

Some of the larger items and less interesting pieces went pretty cheap. I bought a job lot of hammers of every description. As many as I could carry. Every one to tell its tale with shafts sculptured with the blacksmith's hands. Thumb holes and palm grips, all were

He walked round and round the box.

there. It got to the tool boxes — there were several.

'Can I see three pounds?', said a hopeful Auctioneer. 'Two' said somebody. 'Three' came from the back. 'Four' 'Five' 'Six' I pricked my ears up at this amazing response. It did not stop 'Ten' 'Eleven' 'Twelve' — 'Fifteen'. We looked round at the bidders — they didn't look like Blacksmiths. I think the final price was about thirty pounds and that set the going rate. This was 1976 and we couldn't believe it.

At this point Alan our local blacksmith who now does a variety of wrought iron work, walked forward into what was a man made selling ring. A circle in fact. He walked round and round the box with mock expression of looking for something.

'Can I help you'. said the Auctioneer.

'Yis', my blacksmith friend retorted, 'I was lookin for t'hoss — thought it were included in't price'. There was uproar, bystanders were just about falling on the floor with mirth. It took a few minutes for order to be restored and several people had joined our group in conversation. It had been realised that our colleagues were blacksmiths and this in itself created interest.

One rather elegant lady who was obviously a follower of the Barbara Woodhouse animal programmes — do you remember 'Sit't'? approached us.

Looking at my friend's brother who was the farrier, she enquired. 'Tell me' she said, 'Is it true that if you breathe up a horse's nostrils you can talk to it?'

There was no flicker of hesitation in his reply 'Missus' he said, 'It would be as effective as resuscitation through the rectum!' I have got to add that he didn't put it quite this eloquently.

You are wondering who bought the tool boxes? It turned out afterwards that they were from different local authorities setting up craft museums and had open cheques. They got run up (a trick played on people by bidding against them and then dropping out). Well, serve them right. I didn't attend many auctions after that, the writing was on the wall. Between Antique dealers and local authorities what chance did one have?

It is not my intention to dwell too long on collecting old implements. It would be very boring. Suffice to say that I have travelled miles and tried to make our collection an interesting one. You could say that the most boring of all was driving back from Altrincham in Cheshire on the M62 with a horse plough on a trailer.

Talking about antiques there is another interesting story that is worth recording.

Always on the look out for items of interest in local newspapers the following heading caught my eye. 'Small Museum to Close.' I read on — it was a small private collection of local domestic and farming items which had been run by a village Blacksmith at Hunmanby. It did not pay its way and the owner was considering ways of disposing of it. The article went on to say that the owner was engaged in a lot of Ecclesiastical wrought iron work and was also interested in vintage motorcycles. At the time I was the proud owner of a 1958 Triumph Speed Twin. Well, what was I waiting for? I needed exhibits, and sacrifices have to be made. I didn't have spare cash to buy with anyway.

I rang up with my proposition. An agreed amount of museum pieces as a straight swop for my bike. After a look at the bike and examining the situation it was agreed. In fact we got a good deal because the owner said we could have anything that he didn't wish to keep or anything that hadn't been loaned.

I was luckily able to call upon my sons and son-in-law to help move some of these items — there were even some battered old horse implements stored in a field.

What a marvellous start. It was a miracle really because my wife

Ann with almost the view of some bank managers had said 'It's all very well Tony but I think you will need something else beside Shire Horses. Some of the wives might be more interested in some old domestic items.'

She got her wish, and using what we already had as a base, (I tell visitors our unwanted wedding presents), we managed to put together our interesting cottage museum. For some of the items that have either been loaned to us or given can I take this opportunity to say thank you to the donors. One item is a beautiful Christening gown.

In 1978 I bought the old Ruston Proctor Threshing machine. It was from a farm sale held at Scalby High Mill in September. It belonged to a man called Pickering and the whole amusing incident has already been described in my previous book 'At a price that's very nice'. Threshers are bulky things and usually stood outside and were well sheeted down. Well, ours survived this for a year or two but a machine that age (it was made in 1890) starts to deteriorate rapidly if not properly protected from the elements.

In the early 1980's I decided to build it a home. Again with the help of my sons and son in law Rob, we built the shed it now stands in. Using all second-hand and re-claimed materials we assembled the leg sections and top frame. Then using our tractor front end loader which, by adding a length of telegraph pole we managed to make into a crane. Glenn did the driving and perched the five angled steel roof trusses on top of the poles with infinite precision.

Another marvellous D.I.Y. building which I designed from materials on hand and built (what do they say?) on the cheap. Well I have a talented family and some talented friends and this is reflected in our achievements.

The only building we had when we came, apart from the small range of stone buildings, was the old pole hay barn, now reclad and refurbished as the Video Studio.

My wonderful constant daily satisfaction is to walk round in the evening and count the years in terms of renovated buildings, vehicles and implements, carefully planned and low profile new buildings, tidy yards and walls, attractive fences. There has not been a minute wasted.

CHAPTER FOUR
DEVELOPMENTS

By 1982, after extensive restoration by ourselves, the family had leased Rigg Hall Farm just a few hundred yards to the North of us and linked by a track known as Riggs Lane. At one time it was owned by the Overseer of the Freeholders, Robert Mainforth.

Our elder daughter Shirley and her husband Rob, together with David our eldest son and his wife Liz having divided the house into two, had moved in with their respective families.

We had planned a shared enterprise to make the running of our eventual Shire Horse Farm a family affair.

One of the first jobs was to clear the lane of badly overgrown thorn bushes and brambles and open it out for a vehicle. This we did and the then National Park Ranger organised some employment training scheme labour and fenced it along one side to prevent grazing cattle from eroding the hedgebank further, and restricting the width.

The idea was to make a clear access for our eventual visitors and partly protect walkers from livestock.

At that same time the elderly neighbours of ours who owned the land, had decided to retire from their small farming activities and rent the land to a tenant.

It soon became obvious that so far as we were concerned things were going to take a turn for the worse. Within weeks a bull appeared on the lane. It just happened at that same time that we got a visit from the Park Uplands Management Scheme organiser. He had come to examine the work and said he thought some attempt should be made eventually to rebuild the old wall. He spotted the bull — 'What's that doing on this road?'

I must admit by any stretch of the imagination I wasn't happy with it either, whatever type of bull it may be. My daughter who was expecting a baby had a toddler and a young daughter just starting school — she had to walk her through this lane pushing a buggy.

'I will look into the bull question' said the Parks Officer, 'leave it with me.' He was as good as his word, the bull got moved, thank goodness, but more was to come. Times were changing and so was our quiet existence.

It was a great help having the family close by and our lovely grandchildren. Although I have to be fair and say having them and us! living so close together did create a few problems. Nevertheless problems apart we would welcome them all back tomorrow. Shirley our daughter and family are now all living in New Zealand.

She had to walk through this lane pushing a buggy.

Back to the present. At about this time we were busily engaged carrying out a two phase tree planting scheme designed by the North York Moors National Park Landscape Architect. It was part of a voluntary scheme set up to encourage the planting of more trees in the area. From our point of view it was to help enhance our future development plans and also to act on a suggestion by the Parks Officer's assistant, that trees would provide screening for cars being parked. I thought that was good forward thinking.

Well time was moving on and it was fast becoming a not how but when situation. Did we have enough to offer the public, did we have the layout attractive enough and above all could we offer good value for money?

In fact, were we ready to open our doors and how much should we charge. I decided to consult with the National Park and the people who were engaged in development and promotion.

A meeting was soon arranged and three of the Parks Officers came to the farm to offer expert advice — two of them I have already mentioned and had met, and one, the Park Promotions Officer I had not. They were very enthusiastic and helpful and looked round our displays and collection with great interest. In fact I think they were impressed. During the ensuing discussion it was suggested what a wonderful demonstration unit this would make.

I was more than pleased, this was the encouragement that I had been waiting for. 'Well' I said, 'When do we open and are we quite ready?'

The answer was spontaneous, 'Open as soon as you like, you have plenty of interest in your static displays and of course your horses — they will be a tremendous attraction.' The next question was how much shall we charge.

'Well what did you have in mind?', said one.

'One pound for adults and 50p for children I thought.'

They were all agreed that was quite a modest amount and certainly acceptable. Well that was that, a great step in the right direction and the next move was up to me. They wished me the best of luck and again offered any help they could give and went on their way.

I was excited and a bit nervous. This was decision time and I had got to make it work. Well there was no rush. I believe a successful business is only established through creating a good first impression. People have got to go away happy and satisfied. They have got to feel that they have had good value for money, will tell their friends, and more than that, come back again.

I decided it was finishing touches time and the time for a little breathing space and the right opportunity. Opportunities in my view present themselves but you have to grab them.

A friend of mine had got me interested in competition ploughing with the horses. He did the ploughing and I provided the horses, Princess and Nobby and the plough. We had travelled around with them quite a lot and had been featured several times in a black and white photographic souvenirs book. The book was produced to illustrate a day at a very popular annual event 'The Festival of the Plough', held at Epworth, Nr. Doncaster.

This was the Winter of 1983/84. Quite apart from our ploughing activities my mind was now on final preparations. This included trimming hedges, tidying up ditches and some new fencing. Things were going to plan.

The opportunity I had been waiting for came in the shape of a telephone call both unexpected and unpredicted. 'Would you like to join the Committee of the World Ploughing Match horse section?'

I have described this event in a previous book so I won't bore you with details. Suffice to say it was about fundraising and I was being invited to help. You can probably guess the rest — I offered to organise an open day here at the farm and give all profits to the sponsorship fund. The various thank you certificates now hang in our Coffee Shop.

It was a great success, it created a lot of interest and above all it gave me the springboard I needed to get this venture off the ground. I decided Spring 1985. Unfortunately the day although not spoilt, was marred by events on the road and the field adjoining our farm through which the road passes.

Apparently our tenant neighbour was less than happy either about the event, or the fact that people were crossing his rented land. Several people whom I know well, were accosted en route and told to turn back and others were rudely spoken to. Worse was to come, a herd of bullocks suddenly appeared, let in from another field; they were stampeding round followed by a pick-up truck. The road in question is a County Highway and, for centuries, part of what was known as the old Parish Road. Although designated as a green lane, it was once the main and only access to this farm and others. From my own research it was used regularly as the LNER delivery route for their delivery van from Staintondale Station. There should have been no argument as to its status. It goes without saying that I complained to both the owner of the land and to the National Parks Officer. As an avid listener to BBC Radio Four's programme 'Face the Facts' presented by John Waite, I realise how easy it is to be branded as a trouble-maker. In any event how many people can face the facts or even want to? Needless to say I got no replies but did I expect any?

I was determined that these or any other events were not going to deter me from developing my small farm. 'A concept and an ideal.' — Although that wonderful compliment and description was yet many years ahead. The future or the anticipation of the future spurred me on. Giving pleasure gives pleasure, and the thought of running a viable business out of both a hobby and an obsession was enough to shut out some of the discomfort.

The elderly neighbours no longer farmed. The cows had now gone, no longer taken in for the winter and the filthy, muddy field access gate was firmly shut. On a dark winter's night it was to be avoided except by necessity. The elderly neighbours had previously agreed to a cattle grid but that arrangement had been slammed shut as firmly as the gate!

Laugh and the world laughs with you — cry and you cry alone — nothing was going to get me down. Let us look at the lighter side of life. By now we had attended the World Ploughing Match at Horncastle in Lincolnshire. We were placed somewhere in the middle out of a field of thirty or so. It must have rated as the wettest ploughing match ever. Our farming visitors still talk about it!

As that coming winter drew nearer so did the following Spring. We finally opened to the public on Spring Bank Holiday Monday 1985. What a wonderful and rewarding experience. The visitors loved it and we loved our visitors — What nice people and such enthusiasm! It was amazing really because looking back we didn't have such a lot to offer.

It was not so much working what we had to do round the visitors, it was simply working the visitors round what we were doing!

They watched us schooling young horses, putting harnesses on for the first time, and even Graz (Graziella) riding our Shire Horse Stallion round the field. No patio chairs, PA system or demonstrations in those days. No programme, no video studio but a lot of warmth even on a cold day.

We had no signposts to guide the visitors here, it needed a map and a compass to find us, but find us they did. They talked about us to their friends and they brought them to see us. And they are still coming back.

Our success story was born and thriving. I was ecstatic. I called 1985 My Year.

CHAPTER FIVE
AN OMINOUS VISIT

This book is about a planning dispute and of course the background to it. I have tried to describe it as accurately and truthfully as possible. It is not about too many laughs although it is not without its humorous side, but please read on. During our second year into our visitor attraction opening, a few problem areas began to emerge. One of them was of course the gated access already described. Now you have to get a good mental picture of this situation as it existed then, it is nothing like it now.

The gated country road ran across a field adjoining our property but the field did not belong to us. Access to both the field and the road was through a gate. Just inside there was a pond originally, and because of a constantly blocked overflow pipe the pond very often flooded.

At a later date the pond was fenced on both sides after being cleaned and a new overflow fitted. At the same time the gate was moved to a point further away from the pond.

This operation had happened at about the same time this chapter starts and was a blessing. After almost twenty years it seemed like an act of God. Thanks to North Yorkshire County Council.

At the other side of the field was another gate where the road continued on to our property. It was this area where the problem emerged. It was not a man made one. In the summertime when stock were grazing in the field, on a hot day they found shelter by the hedge and trees just outside our property. This in itself was not a problem but to visitors not used to cattle — and a lot are not, it was.

How to move them while opening the gate into our property and keep them clear whilst driving a vehicle through? Quite an ordeal for some people — they all look like bulls!

The answer was staring us in the face. I still had the heavy steel rails purchased for the other aborted plan. A cattle grid would solve the problem and make life easier for all concerned — that included us!

Again, no sooner a word than a deed. With the help of a local builder and a contribution from a tractor excavator we were in business. Concrete was laid, foundations built and hey presto in just one day it was installed. Magic!

Well not quite. It seems we had trespassed once again. what we had trespassed on this time is unclear but it again brought wrath and condemnation and the threat of legal action. Fortunately for us the NFU Regional Secretary was able to pour oil on troubled waters (or should I say turbulent) and bring sanity to bear.

Kipling my friend, 'If you can keep your head.

On the 26th of June 1986 we had a visitor. Up to this day things had been progressing quietly and we were trying to get on with our lives. The enterprise itself was going smoothly and I was feeling very happy. Our small attraction was going to work out and hopefully would become viable. It is not easy getting a business, so far off the beaten track, off the ground. As I said before visitors had to find us first.

There was an air of half expectancy when a different visitor arrived at the farm one day. I found it somewhat disturbing but I can't honestly say why. Some of us will remember telegrams and a telegraph lad on a bike; I can remember the anticipation that sometimes people spoke of, a kind of telepathy perhaps. This was a quietly spoken man. I would say slightly nervous, perhaps he expected a hostile reception.

'Can I have a word with you 'he said, 'perhaps we could go inside?' 'What have I done this time?' Although he didn't look a policeman, I was beginning to think I could get myself into trouble without trying.

The last similar experience to this, had been when a valuation officer had arrived from the Rating Office. He came in a classic white car which was obviously his pride and joy. I am going to relate this story first and then return to our mystery man.

He didn't leave me in doubt — just stuck his hand out, 'I'm the District Valuer', and produced his card. My heart sank. I have got to say that my heart is used to sinking, so much so it has life rafts slung across its bows.

My thoughts raced, 'Don't know about sinking hearts, if he

slap's some rates on this place it will sink the whole enterprise.' 'It hadn't made a bean yet.

This pleasant faced man, taking a sweeping glance round said, 'It has been brought to our notice that you are carrying on a business here and we do not appear to have received a valuation assessment'. I know full well what he meant but were there not mitigating circumstances? 'Well' I said 'We are only open on a limited basis and anyway most of these buildings are agricultural buildings and used for that purpose.' He smiled again. 'Well how limited and how agricultural?' I rather liked his manner.

Immediately I burst forth with my explanation. I told him about my original idea and the plan that put it into operation. I described the work and preparation and of course the breeding of the horses. At this point I emphasised the Ministry of Agriculture's recognition of the breeding of Heavy Horses and the fact we kept a licensed Stallion. Essential buildings and all that. I made a point about the road he had just slowly negotiated with his rather nice motor car. 'Take that road' I said, 'It is all right talking about rates but the road across that field is a County road and who maintains it? — Muggins!' I was getting into top gear. It was easy to talk about carrying on a business', I went on, 'But the cost of trying to maintain that road is a constant burden and I wouldn't care so much if it crossed our land.'

'I must admit', he said looking down at his polished shoes, 'I did wonder if I was on the right track'. I think he was referring to the mud and the cow pats but I had made a good point.

'More than that', I think I must have sounded almost pleading, 'For the amount of business we are doing any further pressure on overheads will see me off.'

'We are not in the business of killing off enterprise, shall we just look around?' he said quietly. With that I showed him round — well, talked him round would be a better description. I think my enthusiasm shone through because at the end of the tour he said, 'I have listened to your story and I am impressed. I seriously believe you are dedicated to what you do, in fact' he went on 'I don't think you really need the buildings or even the horse because with your enthusiasm, you could make your living telling your stories on a Public House car park.'

'Now he said 'I will get my tape and measure all the buildings and stables and make my assessment. In view of what you have told

He did not mention in what capacity.

me, and if you are prepared to let me have a copy of your current balance sheet, I promise you it will be a fair one! He got into his nice classic car and no doubt it was as reliable as his word. One of the old school and a very nice person indeed.

We return to the mystery man. I think the most disturbing thing about this visit, was that, although this caller eventually explained that he was from the National Park office he did not mention in what capacity. He was not particularly forthcoming and both of us (my wife was now present) found him a little bit inscrutable. Despite that, he had quite a pleasant manner.

He started to ask a few questions about the setting up of the enterprise and whom we had originally been in touch with. Also he wanted to know exactly what we did here and when we were open. I had nothing to hide and so I went thread through the needle about the whole situation as I saw it. Oh yes, planning permission had been mentioned but up to now it had been very vague, It was always 'it is thought', or 'In some areas'. 'Nobody', I said 'had ever been specific about which area, although I had pointed out on several occasions I had no objection to applying for change of use for the buildings on the yard. What I did object to, was having to apply for anything that would deprive us of our farm status and turn us into a commercial visitor attraction only'. I had made the point, when is a field not a field?.

What a pity somebody didn't just turn up with a set of planning application forms at the time and offer some advice and assistance on exactly what was required and how the formal application should be made.

Our visitor listened with interest and made a few notes. 'I don't suppose you have any correspondence or copies of anything previously discussed?'

Now it was our turn. My wife left the room and appeared minutes later with a complete file. As an ex-solicitor's clerk, she had it all at her fingertips. It was all there. The correspondence, the reference to site meetings, the help and encouragement, the tree planting schemes and above all the names of all National Park Officers previously involved.

He studied it all very carefully and surprise, surprise, 'Well you certainly seem to have done all the right things' he conceded. Then a remark which stuck the knife in. 'Actually' he said, 'the reason for this visit was an anonymous letter. Somebody has written to say you are using buildings for business use and not paying rates and you are making money charging admission and not declaring your income. In short, defrauding the Inland Revenue'.

We simultaneously exploded!

'Do you mean you have to take notice of mischief making of the worst kind — poisonous anonymous letters?' 'I am afraid so', he said 'They are followed up in exactly the same way as any other complaint we receive.' At least we now knew we had an enemy, unpleasant though that may be. 'Anyway' said the visitor. 'I shall be on my way. Thank you for being so co-operative. I have made a note of all relevant information and I shall now go and follow it up. You will be hearing from me shortly.' When he had gone Ann and I looked at each other. 'What was he then?' I said. Ann considered for a while and answered 'Well I should think he is either a solicitor, or,' laughing, 'A National Park Secret Service Agent!

On the 20th August, nearly two months later we received a letter as promised. It confirmed all that we had said as correct and also that he wanted to confirm planning consent would be needed if we were to open more than twenty eight days in total in any calendar year. He told me to consult his colleague (named) if I wanted to discuss it further.

He also in the letter described our enterprise as a most interesting, educational and tourism resource. Well I concluded we are nearly at the end of our season. I will decide on my future plans and do as he had suggested — discuss it further and find out just where planning consent was needed.

In fact I was contacted by a Parks Officer who visited me on 23rd April 1987. I received a letter from him on the 8th May of that year, but again I found it vague with regard to determining the area or areas in need of planning consent. I have mentioned how easily this could have been resolved at that time, with the simple act of helping to fill in a few forms on site. It is also interesting to note that at that time there was to be no objection from the Area Surveyor with regard to the road and the subsequent high financial cost to me would have been avoided.

CHAPTER SIX
OF DOGS, PANS AND THRUFFERS

As solid as a rock! What a marvellous reassuring ring those few words have. Something to cling on to, something to trust and something to stand the test of time.

It effectively describes one man and his workmanship. A man who, over the years has left his name literally, written in stone all over Staintondale and beyond.

The original old stone buildings which now form the centre-piece of this enterprise, were built in the early nineteenth century and possibly long before. Not many people realise this, but they are basically dry stone walls built from stone with only one square face. The strength of the walls lies in the construction, which was very important. It involved bonding all joints by carefully selecting every piece. There were also pieces called 'Thruffers' referred to in the title, which bonded the inner and outer skin together.

A stone wall is constructed, not just built, and a good stone mason knows exactly where its strength and weakness lies. I have written this chapter about Des, because he has left his trademark well and truly on our buildings. They are there to be admired now, and for posterity. He also taught me a lot about pride in your job and certain building skills that are a thing of the past. Above all he taught me something about stone. He told me that when he started building, and it was nearly all stone buildings at that time, that he worked six days under tarpaulins cutting and dressing stone and six days building. In his early days he said builders were builders. The stone and the timber was on the site and everything was made from it. I rang him because he had been recommended and I was soon to learn why. I told him what I wanted. 'Well now let's see, I shall be at so and so's until next Wednesday and then I have half a day at Cloughton. I have my regulars you see, have to work their little jobs in between. Then there's emergencies'. A pause for thought. 'Can you pick me up at the bus stop at the end of your lane a week on Friday morning, ten past seven?' And then, 'Oh could you get some sand and cement?'

At that time he didn't have his own transport. He carried his tools in his bag and his skills and experience in his head and his hands. It was a laugh from the start that day, he had a marvellous sense of humour and an explanation for everything.

I have never taken to anybody so readily, he called a spade a spade and everything else a bustard! Well, something like that. Work, he was a colossus among men! It seemed to me at that time, that he could be mixing a barrowful of plaster with a shovel in one hand, and plastering a wall with a trowel in the other. Many people will remember this description of him because that is just how he was.

I have been involved in building work for a very long time now, so these comments are from experience and well deserved. 'Right', as they used to say on the building site' Are we having a start?'

The first job we looked at was a broken stone lintel over the barn door. It had the inscription upon it 'R & M 1814'. One Robert Mead no less, head of the Mead family when the 'New' farmhouse was built.

It was cracked right through, and had allowed the stone work above it to slip and push forward.

'Water' said Des looking up at the gutter. 'If these buildings had proper spouts on, the water wouldn't have washed all the mortar out of the joints (pointing) and caused the stone to move' he went on 'No point in repairing these buildings unless you are going to fit new spouting'. When he said things like that, he said it with such conviction, it was advice you ignored at your peril.

At that moment a wasp emerged from the crack in the lintel — followed by another. Des was suddenly more concerned about the appearance of the wasps than he was about gutters. 'That job will have to wait until you get rid of those Kami Kazi (Japanese suicide pilots) Bustards!!' He explained 'There will be a nest full of them Bustards in that wall — thousands of 'em. Get the little Bustards out'. I laughed 'How?' I said, 'Smoke 'em out, burn 'em out, but there is no way we can take that wall out, until they are gone. That nest could be a yard long. What else is on the agenda?'

'Well', I said' I have got some ambitious plans for the creation of a blacksmith's shop, and the old low doorway cart shed would be ideal' I paused 'Well except for the fact that it is very unstable, and the stonework above the old wooden door lintel is bulging out'. 'Let's have a look at that then' said Des. Again he looked up at the verges. 'Same problem!' he commented 'Water's run down the front, it's got into the stonework and then saturated that old beam — be a bit of old ship's timber that!' he went on 'It never dried out properly and that's done the damage — the beam's rotted'. He ran his eyes along and above and then examined the inside. 'The pan (wood wall plate) running along the wall is all bowed out with the wall and rotten too, by the look of it. We shall have to prop those rafters and take it out!' Again a pause whilst he took in the whole situation. 'The whole lot right down to door top level, will have to come down!' 'Whew', I said contemplating a lot of work. 'It can be done' said Des, 'But we shall need a bit of scaffolding'.

My mind was working well at this point and the realisation of creating something I had always wanted, suddenly occurred to me. 'Could you build an archway into it?' I spoke a bit hesitantly because I didn't want to put this man off doing the job.

'Well we would call that a segment, you couldn't really get a full archway in there, but yes I could do it'.

My eyes shone 'That's marvellous. It would really give my blacksmith's shop some character'.

'You will have to make a profile', said our by-now master craftsman (well, in my eyes already) 'Can you do that?'

'No problem at all'. I couldn't wait to get started.

'I'll just have a look at the other walls to make sure we have a stable building before we start pulling down. Don't want the whole lot collapsing on our heads'. He walked round the back of the buildings with the eye of an expert.

"Problem there" he said, `Can you see how badly the back wall has been pushed out? That's because the roof hasn't been tied in and it's pushed the walls apart'.

'What can we do about that?' I enquired.

'Buttress' came the reply 'We build a purpose built buttress against the back wall and stabilise it. It won't go any further'.

I breathed a sigh of relief. It all sounded too good to be true. 'Right, for a start, we shall need to dig out and put a solid foundation in. There will be a lot of weight and pressure, so we don't want any movement'.

I helped in this first operation and after witnessing the type of stone and heavy flagstones selected for this job, I mentally thought it would need an earthquake to move that lot. In fact the more I got to know Des the more I realised that it would take more than a simple earthquake — more on the lines of a nuclear explosion!

The work progressed well and I spent the day carrying stone. It is hard for some people to imagine this, but a seven foot high buttress with a four foot base and something like two foot thick, would take several tons of stone.

Each piece was laid with precision and at intervals bonded into the wall. At last a large piece was accurately cut for the top. Des trowelled on a bed of mortar, 'There, that'll just fit in there'. He dropped it into place — perfect. After pointing (flushing) all the joints he stood back 'That'll never move', he said. 'Not unless somebody drops a bomb', I thought; 'and even then, we could shelter under it'.

That out of the way we turned our attention to the front. By now I had been and hired some scaffolding and we erected that first, Des was as good at taking down as he was at building.

Armed with a long cold steel chisel and his four pound lumphammer he set about it. His forearms were a give-away for the physical effort his work demanded, and he lifted the heavy stones off effortlessly.

'Here catch hold of this' he would say now and again as the scaffold buckled under the weight.

'I'd better lift some down' I said and proceeded to do just that, before the weight did some damage. 'Just stack it all inside the building, we don't want it getting wet'. I laboured away enjoying every minute, as the two of us set about putting the world to rights.

There was a laugh every few minutes as well, as we each swapped a yarn or two. His stories of building in his apprentice days fascinated me — far removed from all the tools and equipment found on a modern building site of today. 'It was all plumb-lines and plumbobs then' said Des. 'No fancy plumb-rules'. (Vertical spirit levels).

I don't want to bore my readers with too much technical detail, but the springing of an arch is a marvellous feat, and one that has been known to man for thousands of years. It is done with a profile or form and this is set in position and built over.

Each segment which forms the arch support is carefully cut and

It's got to last out the
building, said Des.

set out on the profile. The stone selected, Des explained, must be hard and weather resistant. 'You don't want soft sandstone that's going to weather and flake away — it's got to last out the building'.

Each piece of segment was certainly hard. I could hear the ring of the steel chisel as it occasionally deflected from the cut. They looked marvellous just set out in dry form, and the centre key stone, the crowning glory.

Des explained, 'You see the strength of an arch is in the segments and the fact that they are being pushed together by the weight of stone above. The keystone is tapered and of course this means wedge shape. It effectively wedges the segments against each other'. Even now in its dry stone wall form (without mortar) you could have removed the wood profile and it would have stayed in place.

The lovely colours of different stone types are very evident in the arched stone of our Blacksmith's shop. There are shades of blue, red and grey and the brown tints of iron ore, which give away the secrets of its metal content.

By now as the days had gone by I had spent some time and got rid of the wasps nest — no need to make too much of that episode, but like my builder friend I was very relieved to see the back of them. Now we could set to work replacing the broken Mead lintel.

This man's confidence in the skills of his craftsmen predecessors never ceased to impress me.

'All about cantilevers' he had said, 'Have you got an iron bar and a prop about 8 feet long?' He went on. 'I'm going to pin the wall whilst we take out that lintel, by supporting one important stone with the bar and prop'.

He knew exactly which stone, and within the space of a few minutes we put his cantilever theory to the test. I was amazed. No modern Acrow props and screw jacking system, no complicated scaffold. Nothing more than one steel bar and prop and a wealth of knowledge and know how.

Again we are talking about supporting two to three tons of stone. The broken lintel removed, the wall was carefully rebuilt with a plain stone lintel and pointed to match in with the existing wall.

The inscribed Robert Mead lintel had to have a home, broken or not, and the opportunity to find it one came not too long afterwards. It is now proudly displayed built into the front of another old cart shed, by this time the area we call our 'Farm hand tool collection'.

This weathered and age-damaged front gable was also under threat of collapse and again, Des to the rescue. 'They want preserving really', he had said at the time of its removal. 'Anything with a date on it!' Well here was the perfect site. A south facing aspect at the front end of a building which is clearly in view to visitors.

I tell the Mead story of the smuggling and the murder trial on a fairly regular basis throughout the summer. We are proud to own Eastside Farm and proud of the previous owners and its colourful history. Life is a sort of circle and each piece is a segment of that circle. This story is very much a chapter of my life really, and could be described as an instalment of one's autobiography. To preserve and protect the past has given me a lot of pleasure, and to people like my builder friend, it must have given a tremendous amount of satisfaction. I commend it to posterity.

O yes Dogs! I almost missed this bit of my title. These were timber wall ties really, and when a building was up to the square — that is all four walls of equal height, the pans (wall plates) were laid in position. The dogs, (one at each corner) were laid over them and gable ends built up with the dogs built in. The ends of the dogs were then nailed or spiked into the pan and this prevented the apex roof pushing out the walls.

I wonder if these are the real subject of the expression 'A dog's life'. They certainly couldn't go far and even being chained to a wall would be better than being built into one!

As a footnote to this chapter I also have to credit the lovely stone Inglenook inside the house, to this true village craftsman.

CHAPTER SEVEN
THE BOMBSHELL

The purpose of this book is to examine our planning problem in retrospect. Everything, they say, is easier with hindsight. We now return to the plot and looking again at the background, and the disturbing influences that led to our many months of harassment and trauma. This enterprise had settled down to almost a routine and enjoyable situation. There had been a few incidents but turning the other cheek and an occasional symbolic gesture — if you know what I mean — had proved effective.

Our problem now was visitor numbers. We were running at a loss and struggling. How do you get visitors interested and more important, how do you make sure they find you?

Looking at the funny side, although I am not sure the visitors found it funny, we actually had some people drive all the way from Hornsea to visit us. After driving round the area for two hours, they trundled all the way back to the Tourist Information Centre at Hornsea to complain they couldn't find us.

Signs were what we needed but where and how? I decided to take the initiative and a gamble. The A171 was close by — our nearest main road. My plan was simple and effective. I would make a few signs, have them professionally painted in brown and white and erect them myself. I would then write to the County Surveyor and ask for deemed consent (something I had read about) to allow them as temporary signs pending an application for a more permanent arrangement. So far so good, as I effectively put plan A into operation. (The world loves a trier!) Well it certainly helped, and encouraged by the fact I had received no response to my letter I felt rather smug.

It lasted throughout the whole of that first season and as promised in my letter to the County Surveyor, I dutifully removed them at the end of September.

Painted in brown and white and erect them myself.

Unknown to me there was a stirring in the bushes. I had been rumbled. But by who? The following Spring I again erected my 'Temporary Signs' and at the same time sought the help of N.Y.C.C. Traffic Signs Department for either a form or procedural advice. I had written a letter.

Before a reply was received other events were unfolding. A telephone call from a neighbour brought bad news. He had sighted a gang of N.Y.C.C. workmen with a small truck removing and taking away my signs. I was furious (again) and after all my diplomacy and overtures.

A friend of mine who had an ear to the ground, told me where they might be, and whom I should contact. It did not take me long to follow this information through.

I was less than polite. 'Do you realise those signs are temporary and with assumed deemed consent.' Better be careful I thought. 'And more than that, they were expensive signs and I shall hold you responsible for damage!' He listened, so I pushed on, 'I have written to County Hall for permission pending a formal application — you had no right to remove them!' He turned out to be a very nice man and I think he sympathised.

'I will return them to you personally and I can assure you there is no damage.' He added confidentially 'One of your neighbours is making trouble for you every time you put a sign up, we get anonymous telephone calls. In fact', he went on 'We had one this morning to say that you had clagged one to a road signpost.' Well here was a clue, who would use a word like 'clagged?'

He was as good as his word and later that day he returned the signs to me. My assumption was correct, he was a nice bloke and it was reassuring to know that there are human faces behind a lot of bureaucracy.

As proof of my integrity, I quote a reference from a reply card dated 16th November 1988. The card read 'Thank you for your communication which shall receive attention, as and when staff resources permit.' It was of course the reply to my letter regarding permanent traffic signs and the necessary procedural advice.

Was it a joke? I decided to telephone and find out.

Again I made contact with a human being — another helpful person who explained all. 'Oh it meant what it said, in fact at this moment in time we are really struggling staff wise.'

I was amazed 'So we just have to wait do we?', I said 'How long before the situation changes?' 'Could be weeks', he replied and then 'What was it about?'

He listened intently to my account of events, I think we even managed a laugh.

'As I see it you don't really have a problem. All you need is a supportive letter from the Yorkshire and Humberside Tourist Board confirming you are a member, and of course that you are a bona fide visitor attraction. If you accompany that with a plan of where you already had the signs, we will do the rest.'

I really couldn't believe my ears. It was the Eighteenth of November and my birthday. 'You have made my day, my year, and the rest of my life. In fact you have set a precedent, because this is the first really helpful local authority department I have experienced.'

It was not to last. My euphoria was to be torpedoed once more.

Weeks went by and I heard nothing. I had submitted a compelling and supporting letter from YHTB together with a plan almost immediately, but now it was another new year, and another new season approaching. We desperately needed those signs. I decided to telephone and ask for my friend in court. It was a rather subdued voice that eventually answered.

'Not good news I'm afraid. You need some help'. The last bit sounded ominous. 'Do you know a County Councillor who would support you?' There was a brief silence. 'I can't really say any more than that — sorry but your application met total opposition. I wish you the best of luck.'

How many roads must a man walk down? another song as always, sprang to my mind. Well I thought inwardly 'As many roads as it takes, I am not giving up.'

The ideal Councillor I thought, had got to be someone with a vested interest in the management of Yorkshire and Humberside Tourist board and also, in the County Council. I knew exactly who. I wrote him a letter. I had chosen the right person and a detailed enquiry into the full circumstances was instigated. It was not to my advantage and bearing in mind various comments, perhaps, I should have taken action at the time.

The reply I received referred to — surprise, surprise 'Planning approval and road signs — or the unauthorised use of!'

Well it was fair comment to a point, but only to a point. I was still in the dark as to exactly what needed planning consent. And since the last official visit by a planning officer I had heard nothing.

My recollection of the last visit was one of grave concern about the County Road which served our property. The track across the field. I had applied to the Countryside Commission for some help towards maintenance, only to be referred back to the National Park Authority, who had been unable to help.

More than that, in 1987 I had contributed to the Countryside Commission's Countryside Review Panel with my own views and objectives. This was for European Year of the Environment and a subsequent publication, 'New Opportunities for the Countryside.' Needless to say it was about roads and access, and I expressed the view very strongly that I should be getting some help maintaining this County Road. To start with, it was not on my property and yet I had maintained it for almost eighteen years at that time.

The incredible amount of deterioration during the winter by monster agricultural vehicles was devastating. These were vehicles sometimes many times the weight of a motor car and almost twice as wide. And again nothing to do with our enterprise.

You may well wonder what all this is leading up to? Well it is really quite simple. I had told the planner on his last visit that if the County were prepared to do something about the road, then I would consider looking at the planning issue.

'What is the point', I had said 'In encouraging development here when all we get is complaints about the track across that field (County Road) not to mention hostility from the tenant of the land. I must add that both tenant and owner had refused point blank by letter, to help with maintenance. Did they even want us using it? Well certainly the hostility was to continue as the following paragraphs will reveal.

1989 was a Summer of Sunshine. A recorded figure of 83 days when the temperature exceeded 70^0F. This was against a national average of 52 days.

Well sunshine for some. But it seemed, for Staintondale Shire Horse Farm clouds were already gathering.

The season had started well and we were all in high spirits. Some of the signs had gone of course, but visitors were all ready coming back for repeat visits — and telling their friends. Our growth might be slow but it was encouraging.

My concern for this enterprise has been of a protective nature. I had no wish to either destroy or even threaten our lovely environment. We have lived here now, as I write these chapters for twenty four years. This has been a lifelong commitment to perfection. A rose to grow, a rose to cherish.

You can imagine therefore, the effect of a telephone call from a Yorkshire Post newspaper reporter on Friday morning of June 9th — it was devastating.

My wife Ann had answered the telephone and a brief conversation ensued. I saw her face drain of colour. She handed it over to me 'It's a Yorkshire Post reporter'.

A voice spoke, 'Hi Tony it's Steve here, how are you?' It turned out that we had already been in contact a year or two previously. That is the good thing about Press relations they are always there and I have always been willing to co-operate. Publicity to me is vital for survival and a friend in the press is worth a lot.

None more so than now. The question hit me like a stone 'What are you going to do about the enforcement action being recommended to the North York Moors National Park Development Control Sub Committee?' he went on, 'I just mentioned it to your wife.' No wonder she turned pale. What was he talking about? At last I found my tongue 'What enforcement action?' 'Well', said my reporter friend 'Apparently you are operating without planning permission and your enterprise is causing problems.' 'Well that's news to me, what sort of problems?' 'You mean you know nothing about this order, or its consequences?' 'Nothing', I spoke with incredulity.

'Well here are a few things you should know. For starters I quote, they are saying that the farm is seriously detrimental to the character and appearance of the area. And also that the site is inappropriate for intensive tourism use!'

'Don't say any more', I said 'What a damned nerve.' 'Well what do you propose to do?' said the reporter. 'I'll tell you what I am going to do — fight them. It is just not on. This farm is a beautiful place, it has been described many times by visitors as idyllic. The buildings are compact and low profile and everything we do is in the best interests of conservation. So far as inappropriate goes, that's rubbish. Shire Horses and the countryside are this country's heritage. We encourage visitors to share this wonderful situation and from a youngster's point of view it is very educational!' I paused for breath. 'We have also inherited a wonderful history dating from the XIIth century. It concerns a Charter granted to the

Noble Order of the Knights of St. John of Jerusalem. It gave them the freehold of the Manor of Steynton in Blackamor together with other gifts and privileges. Not just for them, but for their heirs and successors forever. Pretty impressive stuff hey?'

I was in top gear by now 'Oh it's very real as recent records show. Pursuant to the Charter granted by King Stephen, the freeholders of the Dale could claim exemption from tithes tolls, and land tax. Also, by virtue of privileges granted by the old Charter, they could claim exemption from serving on juries at assizes or sessions. Robert Mainforth, who was overseer for many years, read the Charter to the Judge in Northallerton when jury men were called from Staintondale. This latter information is from the History, Topography and Directory of North Yorkshire published in 1890.'

Let Battle Commence!

'Sounds quite amazing', said the reporter who had listened fascinated. 'But where do you fit in?'

'I fit in very easily. We are probably one of the few remaining farms with deeds dating back to the Eighteenth century, and which include the manorial rights. As a Staintondale freeholder I shall use them in any way possible — might even don my armour and mount a Shire horse charger. Mind you it would have to be Mascot the Stallion in true Destrier fashion!'

'It's a good story', he said 'Look out for tomorrow's Yorkshire Post!'

An eighteen month planning battle was about to start, with all the relevant acrimony, trauma and at times distress. It was a battle to be won.

CHAPTER EIGHT
CRUNCH MEETING

'Farmer Defends Tourist Venture' headed the report. It was the start of some very supportive press and television coverage that was almost to dominate local news for the next few months. I was very glad of it.

I have got to clarify one point though. I do not regard myself as a farmer even after twenty odd years of keeping various livestock. My career has been a business one, and this farm was purchased originally to start a riding stables.

A farmer is a man who cultivates the land and grows crops to both sell, and feed his livestock. I do not fit this category but I suppose to a Journalist a farmer is a man who lives on a farm. Ah well!

The meeting the report referred to came up the following Wednesday, the 14th June 1989. I did not attend, simply because I was not aware that I could have done so. I soon got very wise to procedure in the coming weeks, and I wonder how many other people are ignorant of their rights?

The following day under a banner headline 'Crunch Meeting on Horse Centre', I was able to read about it. It did not please me. If the evidence put forward as background by the planning officer was as reported, then it was either a fabrication of the facts or the lack of them.

They had stated that we had been inviting visitors since 1976 when in fact we hadn't opened until 1985 and that they hadn't heard from me since 1982.

My records and copy letters would clearly show that we had received visits and held serious discussions with planning officers in June 1986 and again in April 1987. Both I might add, inconclusive and neither of them suggesting the Draconian action now being proposed.

They had also stated, I quote 'lately there had been complaints from the Parish Council, particularly concerning the narrow and steep access to the site.' I must confess this latter paragraph pleased me even less. Who were these people, who were complaining and why? We had been operating for four years without any hint of a problem, and certainly no reports of any accidents. Besides why not complain to me? I concluded other forces were at work — again.

It might be worth adding at this point that this area is becoming increasingly dependent on Tourism, and cars coming down that lane were a welcome sight to some people. The report concluded with a decision taken at the meeting that North Yorks Moors members were to visit the farm and meet Mr. Jenkins before deciding what action to take.

Well that meeting on site came the following month, and by now we had received some wonderful television coverage of the dispute. I had been interviewed live on our attractive stable yard, which was as usual a mass of summer colour, flowers and foliage. Our tubs and hanging baskets are the envy of our visitors and have won us endless awards. Add to this our very tidy and well maintained stone buildings and adjoining grass paddocks and you have a mental picture. The interviewer was asking questions. 'They say your enterprise is detrimental to the Environment. What do you say to that?'

I swept my eyes round in a panoramic gesture and pointed.

'Look around you,' I said. 'This is a beautiful place and we put endless time and energy into keeping it that way.'

The cameras took in every detail focussing on flower heads and greenery. The effect was a kaleidoscope of mellow stone and bright summer colour.

I think that question was suitably dealt with.

The final question. 'It's going to be a long battle then Mr. Jenkins?'

'It's going to be a long b——y battle,' I replied. Later I saw the piece on television, I could see why the presenter looked a bit startled. Still I meant it. They hadn't shown me much mercy.

The day of the meeting dawned and we had prepared for it. Although acrimony was possibly in my thoughts at no time during discussion did I let it show. Politeness and good humour costs nothing.

We had placed a bowl of lovely sweet peas on a table in the ladies toilet.

The meeting itself I regarded as an inquisition. I felt I was being tried for treason. My almost lifelong efforts were under threat and my well received and popular enterprise was being doubted. There has got to be a thread of Kiplings 'If' running through this story because it kept my head above water. I am going to quote a line or two I thought relevant.

'If you can trust yourself when all men doubt you, and make allowance for their doubting too.'

'It's going to be a long b----y battle.'

'Or being hated, don't give way to hating.

Or being lied about, don't deal in lies.'

The planner was again quoting his version of the background. I was biting my tongue. My adviser had said, 'Do not get involved in arguments, just listen.'

He (The Planner) was now talking about the access and especially the part of the County Road that was the infamous track across the field. To me he seemed to be implying that this was private property, and I was using it without authority. I could have been wrong.

He went on 'Mr. Jenkins has been demanding that the owners pay for the maintenance of the road.'

I could contain myself no longer. I found it so emotionally distressing that I broke down. I was choked up and found that in trying to defend myself, I was making a mess of the situation. Something I wanted to avoid. My adviser excused my predicament and took over.

What I had wanted to really say, was that this was a lie. Even more poison was being purported by forces unknown. What I had asked for, was a responsible arrangement to make other users of the road contribute to the maintenance. If they felt that any rent they paid the owners of the land put the responsibilities on the Landowner, then so be it. I had written a letter to this effect which was passed on to one of the tenants. It received an immediate rebuff.

I had felt very annoyed at the time because not only had I maintained the road over all the years, but in the early 1970's I had a contractor level it, stone it and then, I even hired a full size road roller from Scarborough Borough Council to make a first class job of compacting it.

In retrospect I now realise that I was making a rod for my own back. This was a County Road No. WY407G and maintainable at Public expense — facts I was not aware of all those years ago. The County Council were in fact opting out of their responsibilities.

One winter's day I had seen my efforts destroyed, as a shuttle of tractors and muckspreaders had turned the road into an unrecognisable quagmire. Mr. Planner you stuck a knife in me that day! The meeting continued and as Councillors looked round, I made an excuse to go and compose myself and then entertain my visitors.

It was July and quite busy. Each open day I give talks and demonstrations and today was no exception.

I knew we had a lot of supporters present and I wasn't going to let them down. The show must go on. Soon back to my usual good natured role as host, I quickly established contact and a very appreciative audience listened intently. Some of them I know, were all for giving these visiting Councillors a piece of their mind. In fairness I have got to say that quite a few were both sympathetic and supportive. Others were there either to pay lip service or line up in opposition. I was learning.

The site meeting dispersed and our day continued as normal. Several of the Councillors stayed on to look round our enterprise and seemingly enjoyed it. It would be fair to say that one or two of them were genuinely impressed and pledged their support. This I found very reassuring because I did realise the value of someone actually speaking on my behalf at the next meeting of the planning sub-committee. One comment made to me that day I did not like. It was to this effect 'Oh I think you will get approval eventually — but you will have to be seen getting your backside kicked!' Someone arrogant enough to ignore the distress and trauma that myself, my wife and staff were going through and stupid enough to think I would concede to being made a scapegoat — I think not.

It was another month now to the next meeting and this was to be held at the North York Moors National Park offices at the Old Vicarage Helmsley on Wednesday August 9th 1989. Support for this venture was now flooding in and many old campaigners were giving me the benefit of their experiences. It was pretty obvious that the park planners were not exactly flavour of the month.

With such wonderful and overwhelming public concern for the future of this enterprise I felt invincible. My strength was the appreciation and encouragement people gave me from all walks of life and all parts of the country.

In the next few months exciting events were to take place and the considerable interest this would provoke left me in no doubt about the outcome.

A bonus came in the shape of two other Councillors who contacted me. One rang to apologise for not being at the site meeting but wanted to come and see me. The other to send copy of letter addressed to the Chairman of the forthcoming meeting. It was very supportive and explained that this particular Councillor would be on holiday and unable to attend. Well at least we had friends in Court. I decided to strengthen my defences. There had been a lot of misunderstanding and doubt about the background to this development and I realised from the attitude of some people that they were not conversant with the facts.

To counteract this I decided to copy some of the relevant correspondence and send it to members of the committee prior to the meeting. The truth, the whole truth and nothing but the truth.

CHAPTER NINE
THE SHIRES GO MARCHING IN

What exactly did we have at our disposal that could create the biggest impact and draw attention to our plight. And how do we publicise our outrage and anger at what we considered to be Bureaucracy gone mad? These two questions had an obvious answer — It was big, it was heavy and it was impressive.

We planned our next move like a military operation — it was to be our *coup de grace*, well a blow for justice anyway. On the morning of the meeting we would take our plough pair Princess and Nobby to Helmsley. This mother and son team were very much part of our family and after all, their future was at stake too.

As luck would have it we had some friends staying with us from Batley and they were very enthusiastic supporters. We decided that the civilised way to approach this offensive was to have a pow wow — well we had a barbecue! We then planned our morning strategy. At the crack of dawn we would box the horses and head North for Helmsley.

Soon our plans were taking shape. The brass mounted plough gear was being burnished and the brasses polished — we would make an impression come what may. Sleep didn't seem all that important. My Senior Assistant Hilary and her willing helpers soon got caught up in the infectious enthusiasm. What an impressive show of defiance. It was hard work but the farm motto 'Nothing by halves' inspired the operation. Agincourt was to be re-enacted outside the precincts of Helmsley Castle.

As the glow of the charcoal faded and the last of the food consumed, our sights were on the morning and the job we had to do. It would soon be 6am.

It was a typical grey start to the day and we drove through a patch or two of rain. Well, did it matter, it was a grey day for us anyway — well was it? We were going to change all that! Our plans and timing were on schedule. Princess and Nobby were all prepared and groomed and travelled comfortably in the trailer.

We arrived at Helmsley early and eagerly observed an almost empty car park — we could choose our best vantage point and it didn't take long. The trailer was backed into place — front facing the main road. After all this was a protest demonstration.

We carefully arranged the placards around our vehicle and trailer 'Save the Shire Farm' and, in the case of our horses 'It is our future that is at stake as well'.

Our friends started to get a petition going just as soon as people were about. It was amazing how many people had heard of us and indeed how many had actually visited the farm.

We didn't start to harness the horses — that was to come later. In the meantime they were stood side by side in the extra large trailer contentedly munching at their hay nets.

Time was steadily passing and everybody was in high spirits. The atmosphere was of great expectation and the ever increasing interest in our demonstration very rewarding. We felt the world was on our side.

At last the big moment came. Time to get the horses out and start to gear them up. We have a particularly interesting set of plough gears, the backbands were made in Scotland something over 100 years ago. These together with a gleaming pair of black highly polished collars with nickel hames created a feast for the eyes.

We carefully put it on the horses — collars first, then blinders (blinkers) and then backbands.

I should add that collars in this part of the country are called barfen's. A set of gleaming polished steel plough chains came next, followed by the coupling together of the horses.

A crowd had gathered as you can just imagine and one older man who had watched the proceedings with the eye of an expert, said 'An when you've got 'em yoked, you want to hang b . . . .y plough on and go 'an plough 'em up!'

At that moment a smiling friendly face appeared. It was the Councillor who had missed the site visit but had come to see me at the farm later. 'I have just bought the sugar lumps I promised'. It was a promise of unequivocal and long lasting support. Something I was to realise the value of later. It was not my original intention actually to drive the horses with the plough lines. For one thing they were not used to main roads and the volume of traffic and for

There was no one more proud than me that day.

another I did not wish to cause a traffic hazard. However, events like the support of the horse era gentleman and spurred on by my own confidence and determination, I decided I would if necessary, drive them right up to the door of the planning office.

I turned their heads towards our target 'Get up Nobby, c'mon Princess! 'I gave a click of my tongue and drove them on to the highway. We were on our way. There was no one more proud than me that day. The horses looked magnificent — just imagine the picture. Two majestic horses almost a perfect match. Feather washed out white and flowing like driven snow. The black highly polished leather a backdrop to the gleaming brasses and polished hames. What a memorable experience.

Hil and Sarah walked outside their heads for safety but the horses never faltered. You would have thought they worked in the middle of a busy main road all their lives.

People were stopping in their cars to offer encouragement. Shopkeepers were leaving their shops to come over and offer their support — even cash, would you believe? That day for a brief period, Helmsley came to a halt.

As we approached The Old Vicarage which was the N.Y.M.N.P. Headquarters we were besieged by what was later described as 'World Press'.

Television Crews, Camera-men, Journalists, Supporters — everybody. What a reception! I was told by one reporter that he had been to the offices to tell one particular planning officer what was going on outside and his colour had literally drained away.

Following this meeting lots of letters of support were coming from all over the country. Our press coverage had now reached the Nationals. A Daily Mail three quarter page article was headed, 'Farmer calls on Horse Power in fight for his Livelihood.' It was followed by a title heading 'How Princess and Nobby won the day in the Shires'. This was Thursday August 10th 1989. The reporter described the action — 'Two mighty shire horses clip-clopped into action yesterday to help their owner with a reprieve for his business!' It referred of course to our taking the horses to the planning meeting.

What a marvellous boost to our moral and our defences! It was

How Princess and Nobby won the day in the Shires.

later picked up and used by Horse and Hound as another victory for Horse Power.

The public loved it and the support flooded in. This was reinforced by more coverage on local television of the day at Helmsley.

The actual meeting, although described as a reprieve, to me seemed little more than a stay of execution. It had become increasingly obvious, that the underlying problem was our old adversary, the old Parish road which ran across our neighbours' field. However my trump card was still to play.

The Planning Officer had spelt it out. 'The access road to the farm itself was unsuitable in its present form and there was no land available to improve it.'

In other words they were not prepared to take steps under their statutory powers to provide for, either passing places or the widening of this country road WY 407G. One Councillor at the site meeting had voiced an opinion that they should and could. Was there even a solution to the problem? It is rather ironic because at the time it could easily have been overcome by a voluntary offer of allowing a couple of modest passing places on the field by the owners of the land.

The mood of the meeting itself was one of guarded optimism. Our friends in court were the councillors who vehemently supported what they described as an ideal low key development and just what the park needed.

The planners, visibly shaken by the amazing public support and events outside were anxious to make public that they thought a solution could be found.

I sat poker faced, my cards were still close to my chest.

The Chairman of the Committee eventually had recommended that the matter be adjourned for six months and that further talks should be arranged to try and find a solution. Well at least a breathing space, and I owe a debt of gratitude to several Councillors who fought hard for my survival. I should say, one in particular who gave an impressive interview on my behalf for a local television channel.

I felt very strongly that I was being deprived of my legal and established right of access. To this end, I even obtained a copy of the Enclosures Award. It was addressed to the several proprietors (Freeholders) of lands or other Hereditaments within the Township or Lordship of Staintondale. It was dated 3rd October 1829.

Downdale Road was set out and awarded a breadth of forty feet and it extended through allotments (land) to an ancient road leading down the Dale on the East of John Mainforth's old enclosure. The WY 407G! I have done my homework but the law is a ponderous thing and we are not going to live forever! Right now, I needed a road and within my grasp I thought I had the answer. Just a few years earlier I had purchased some land adjoining our property which was bordered by another section of this old County Highway. It would be possible, although expensive, to swallow my pride for the time being and look seriously at creating a brand new access road to the farm, something like 300 yards of soil excavation and new stone foundations. This was of course subject to approval by the planners, and satisfactory public and vehicle access rights being established. I was about to play my hand.

Time was slipping by now, and the season had ended as usual at the end of September. We only had six months, so I decided that I would take the initiative and start applying pressure to get the proposed talks under way. Needless to say (would you believe) and I am a prolific letter writer, it still took until November, but at last a meeting on site was arranged. There had been some adjustments to staff structuring at the National Parks Office. I had been informed of this, and I was looking to establish a good relationship from the onset.

The new planning officer duly arrived at the farm, this time it was a woman. I was not to be particularly disappointed, but I must admit an early remark about an inappropriate site, did put me on guard.

My attitude has never faltered. This is my life, it is my world and this development belongs here. The horses were practically all born here, and it is where they belong.

It is not some kind of amusement arcade that can be moved around and pitched somewhere for its best volume of customers — and cash. If making money were my only purpose in life, then as a businessman I could have thought of a million better sites.

Quality of life was the reason for my buying this farm in the first place and quality of life is my reason for fighting to hang on to it. And which is more, it is this quality that endears the public to it and what makes it so unique. They show respect and appreciation and we respond to their support.

CHAPTER TEN
ONEROUS CONDITIONS LEAD TO A BLOCKADE

Putting my prejudices behind me I had put forward my proposal for a new road. We had walked the fields overlooking the farm and the plan that I had suggested received a favourable response. The Planning Officer took the view that a new road, almost parallel to the established access was acceptable and would have less impact on the landscape. I agreed.

We discussed other aspects of the planning application and, for the very first time in over ten years somebody actually sat down with me and produced a set of forms. More than that, actually explained planning procedure and paved the way for open discussion on which areas were involved. I was impressed. Passing places were mentioned on Downdale Road but certainly with no particular emphasis. It was thought, (convenient phrase), that Highways wouldn't be asking too much! The main access point would be subject to the Surveyor's report, and safety would be a consideration. I thought that sounded reasonable.

The retrospective application would be submitted in January and subject to approval, the Surveyor's report and conditions would follow in due course.

I did wonder why the latter couldn't have been submitted to me for approval before the meeting. After all I was footing the bill! At the meeting there was an air of relief — was this much publicised and possibly embarrassing dispute about to end?

The Planner presented the case well. She referred to 471 letters of support — even to the extent of quoting very favourable comments from them and some criticism of planners! She also said that only one letter of objection had been received and it was from a neighbour of Mr Jenkins. She read it to the meeting. The Area Surveyor had not yet made a recommendation, but she thought he would be stipulating certain improvements to Downdale Road and the access point to our property off the road number WY407G. All of which we were to pay for. I am still at a loss to understand why this could not have been dealt with within the six month period recommended by the Chairman at the August meeting. The Planners then tried to impose a condition that approval be only granted to me personally and was not to be transferred. One Councillor stood up and said that was grossly unfair and said that at least my sons be named as successors. Another said that the sort of press publicity this case was attracting was making them a laughing stock.

In the event my business was seriously devalued by a stipulation that it could only stay in family ownership. I was there, and I listened to the report with calculated apprehension. Well it sounded fine but some of the conditions about to be imposed were vague on account of them being conspicuous by their absence — what would they amount to and how much would they cost? We had to wait and see. We were now into 1990 and another season was looming large.

I was starting this season with a new assistant and I was looking forward to something less traumatic. How wrong can you be?

Before we opened to the public the full conditions attached to the planning application arrived. We had won, to quote my adviser a 'Pyrrhic Victory'.

'Onerous' — one word fitted the situation. Was this the straw that broke the camel's back? I read and re-read. The cost was escalating before my eyes.

At almost sixty years of age I must admit I was calculating how long it would take to earn this sort of money, and more than that, was it really worth the effort?

'Oh well Kipling old lad' (with apologies) I quote, 'If you can make a heap of all your winnings and risk it on one turn of pitch and toss!' I intended to stay in business come what may, so a few more weeks of argument and objections were acceptable. I was not giving in now.

I wrote a strong letter of protest and set out my objections in no uncertain manner. My planning adviser observed 'It seems that they have decided that if they can't get you one way, they will get you another!'

Several weeks of discussion took place and of course by now, the cat was out of the bag. A new road was in the offing and it did not suit everybody. In fact people who had pledged support suddenly turned against us. People in our immediate vicinity as well. Why this sudden change of attitude? It began to smack of conspiracy, I found it disturbing. To me it seemed ominous. Somebody had loved to see us fight but hated to see us win.

Stopping the use by visitors of the County road across our neighbours field, would have effectively put us out of business.

Now we looked like surviving with our alternative access. There had already been one solicitor's letter saying that the proposal was ill advised and inappropriate and warning of the consequences. It had been rejected emphatically by all parties including the County Secretary as being irrelevant.

This was not to be the end of this matter and a closing of ranks became apparent. I have referred earlier to the purchase of this land which gave us another access to County road No. WY 407G. Although at the time of purchase and immediately afterwards thoughts of a new access road had been envisaged, but of course the cost was prohibitive. Having said that we had mown a strip right across it which had become known as 'Tony's landing strip' one summer.

The story continues and it is with unmitigated sadness that I have to record this next episode of developments closely associated with the planning dispute.

Throughout the entire period I had tried to conduct myself in a dignified manner. Our protests although effective had been by demonstration and not belligerent confrontation.

Many times I have been provoked and even lied about over certain issues, but to lose your temper is to lose the argument. Having lived here for over twenty years I had taken this village and most of the community to my heart.

It was now obvious that some small element was intent on poisoning this situation and it hurt.

On Wednesday 9th May 1990 the sound of heavy metallic clanking and banging could be heard. It was a summer's evening and still quite bright. I went round to the front of the house to see where this intrusion of noise was coming from. I did not have to look far. The County road which I have referred to previously, and which is known locally as 'The Stripe' was being posted on both sides. Alternate short and long heavy stakes were being driven into the ground with a mechanical post knocker. The width of the track was being restricted to a bare minimum and passing or re-passing of vehicles rendered impossible.

I was shell shocked. This was an attack from a very different angle and totally unexpected. The scene was one of being imprisoned in your own home, as this stockade like edifice took shape.

This lovely old ancient meadow was witnessing an act of aesthetic vandalism, and I was witnessing desperation of a kind I had not previously encountered. Why oh why, oh why? That night we found sleep difficult and so it was an early next morning, that found me seeking urgent legal advice.

Relief! To a point the law was very much on our side. It seemed that after living here for over twenty years we had an easement which gave us private rights to use any width of access we may find necessary along that County road.

If this could be proved to have been established for over forty years, then there was basically no action that could threaten it. I knew from my own records and from a History, Topography, and Directory of North Yorkshire dated May 1st 1890 that we could claim 100 YEARS! The advice I received was compelling — get the posts out and try not to cause any damage or disruption or a disturbance of the peace. If there looks like being any sort of nasty confrontation then you would be wise to call upon the services of a local Police constable.

The last bit sounded ominous — I hoped at least we could behave like civilised people. How to get them out was the immediate problem. It would not be easy.

I had an important site meeting that day. It was to include myself of course, the Planning Officer, the Area Surveyor, the County Secretary and my Architect. Big guns indeed. We walked the gauntlet between the posts, it was a bit like a scene from Custor's last stand.

It was also an embarrassing and daunting experience and one I shall never forget.

What went through my mind, was the timing of this unprecedented action. Was it sheer coincidence that this defiant display had occurred on this day, or? the plot thickens, had there been a leak? When nightmares occur in the day-time and we have had our share of those, logical thoughts give way to doubts and suspicions. I joked about a chainsaw but inside my stomach felt sick.

We were walking round the circuit as it were, to explore the possibility of a one way system. It had been suggested by the Area Surveyor. I was trying to make the point that I didn't care what they decided, but must I continue to pay for the maintenance of this old country road?

At the point of the proposed new access a detailed discussion took place.

One of the Surveyor's assistants had previously suggested the wall which partly surrounds an old stackyard, should be removed to widen the existing road towards this proposed new access. I had pointed out that it didn't belong to me and rather than getting involved in compulsory purchases (which he had suggested) could we reach a compromise?

It was this compromise which was now under discussion.

An agreement was reached. The new access road would be located 20 metres North of the South West corner of our property which coincided roughly with the existing access. In addition the Public Highway WY 407G had to be widened to 5 metres at my expense and subsequently surfaced. The road widening was to be carried out within the existing public highway, which included the verge.

The one way system was left as an option but it was later dropped. One way systems are fine whilst everybody is travelling in one direction. We did not have this much control on the old existing County Highway! Well so far so good, I was quite happy with this development and throughout, all discussions and suggestions had been amicable and friendly. This part of the conditions, although costly, I decided would improve our image. People paying admission expect a tidy approach road and first impressions count. I had great plans for it all ready. Wide grass verges, a line of trees and daffodil bulbs!

As time has gone by, we have created a very impressive driveway approach which has won us praise and admiration from many sources.

Well that was that. They were on their way, and I was left with the posts. They were a couple of foot at least, into the ground and we couldn't even move them fractionally. I telephoned all round locally for a J.C.B. but without success. What now? Suddenly I had an idea. Tractor hydraulics — the three point linkage. They could lift a ton or two.

With my young female assistant Jeanette, I drove across to the

Success and a spontaneous hooray!

first post. It was basically an old timber lifting technique using a short twisted chain.

I backed the tractor close up to the post with the transporter platform frame just touching. The chain was dropped over the post to the bottom and wound round the frame. Up we go. Well at first we didn't. Such was the effort needed to pull these posts from the hard ground, the tyres flattened at the base. We held our breath — a burst tyre or? And then slowly, the post started to emerge. Success, and a spontaneous hooray! We never counted the posts but you will see from the illustrations taken from actual photographs — there were a lot.

It took hours, but as time went by my capable assistant Jeanette got very adept with the chain and we made better progress. Our legal advisers had emphasised no damage so we were very careful. We then had to carry them all to the gate and neatly stack them.

As the last one had been pulled out, we had thrown it high into the air together with our hats! It was a defiant gesture and it hadn't gone unnoticed. Jungle drums were sounding and bush telegraph was winging its way.

I am not going to make capital out of the resulting response, but suffice to say there was one. It is only with regret, that I feel justified in recording my account of these events.

It was not the end of an attempt to block our use of this road, and shortly afterwards because this ploy had failed, the field was deep ploughed and laid over, away from the track. The result was a deep void along both sides. Possibly as effective as the posts, but the damage to the environment was incalculable. This was possibly the oldest meadow in Staintondale. There were no previous records of it ever having been ploughed, and we have no reason to believe it ever had.

The Easements created by the Mainforths and the Mead families for hundreds of years had been brought to an end.

Oh yes legal action was possible but that didn't undo the damage. And in any case it seemed so very futile. My new road was going to make a break with history. Robert Mead had purchased East Side Farm from the Mainforths of Rigg Hall in 1770. The stripe, was a stripe across a meadow then!

CHAPTER ELEVEN
A SUMMER OF DISCONTENT

The background to this enterprise as put forward by the planners was, to say the least, extraordinary. I quote item 2.1 'The use of this property as a Shire Horse visitor centre began in the 1970's on an occasional basis without the benefit of planning permission, but by 1982 the level of use was such that the owner was informed that planning permission was required and invited to submit an application.'

Not just extraordinary but quite remarkable. We did not open to the public in any shape or form, limited or otherwise until 1985!

One newspaper reporter told me 'You have already got their backs up (The Committee) with your outspoken comments.'

I must admit my attitude had been less than conciliatory. At that time I had been unable to distinguish friend from foe, and Planners and Planning Committees were to me one and the same thing.

Later I was to discover how wrong I was and how important it was to have the support of some Councillors.

We have now got to the stage when a section 278 agreement arrived through the post. It related to passing places.

Although as I have mentioned already I was aware some kind of passing places were required. I was not prepared for the specification that was to be demanded.

They were of standard Ministry of Transport Highway specification and I was required to submit the necessary plans drawn up by an architect. The responsibilities of carrying out such works was enormous. So far as a planning Committee goes and I do not intend these remarks as derogatory, they are something that just happens. They look harmless enough.

Alongside every highway there are what are known as main services. Mostly they run under the ground and include water, electricity, telephone and in some areas, gas.

It is up to the developer to establish the exact route and plan accordingly. It is time consuming and costly. More than that it can sometimes make excavation in certain areas almost impossible. With my previous building experience I was very well aware what I might be taking on. What we are really talking about, are road improvements usually carried out by civil engineering contractors or local authorities. They wanted me to arrange to carry out these works, take final responsibility and pay. The road in question is known as Downdale Road and it carries mainly local traffic and agricultural vehicles. Well, that was the case twenty four years ago.

From my excellent memory I can categorically state that at that time there were two Ford Anglias, one Transit van, one other car and my own, using Downdale Road. Plus of course a few small tractors in the shape of a Massey Ferguson 35, a grey Ferguson and an old Fordson Major. Add to this an occasional small cattle truck and you have the lot.

How very different in 1990. Well over a dozen privately owned vehicles, large and small delivery vehicles, endless tractor traffic, and not the small variety any more. Plus visitors and tourists of course and not all destined for a visit here.

One farm vehicle had been described by a visitor as of 'Frightening proportions' when met head on once, on this narrow lane.

I am not going to say that such vehicles have no place in rural situations such as this. They are part of the mechanised revolution that has swept agriculture into the 90's. What I am going to say is that it is this same revolution which has changed the nature of the requirement of rural roads.

Not only had the horse and cart gone, but the roads originally developed for them should be gone too.

The economy of the dale is now becoming increasingly dependent on traffic. Local traffic, holiday traffic and business traffic. Downdale Road was long overdue for improvement and yet it had taken my dispute to highlight the fact.

Well I thought, my argument was sound. The cost of these passing places, bearing in mind the unknown and unseen hazards was going to be high. Could be very high.

I weighed it up very carefully and decided a 50% contribution was fair. We open only five months a year and the road improvements would be an all year round benefit for the local community.

I would offer to pay for two of the proposed passing places and put myself at the mercy of the Committee -again. Well after all they had been reasonable and supportive so far. I thought I was getting to know the system.

I am now going to quote from a letter sent to Northern Echo in October 1989, in response to a report published by that Newspaper. It was sent to me by a helpful staunch supporter and sympathiser.

He had written. 'The report gives one the impression that both Hitler and Dick Turpin have come back from the dead and taken up residence at the Old Vicarage, Helmsley. One to say 'stand and deliver or else', the other to force the Shire man out of business. He went on to quote from The Local Government and Encyclopedia on Highway Law, C. Cook, Part IV 1980 Highway Acts:-

'It is the duty of road authorities to keep their public highways in a state fit to accommodate the ordinary traffic which passes or may be expected to pass along them. As the ordinary traffic expands or changes in character, so must the nature of the maintenance and repair alter, to suit the change.'

Well they probably thought, because this was described as a Shire Horse farm, that horse and carts were very much the order of the day. I am referring now of course to the planners and my dispute.

Anyway I was going to pursue my argument, and with

Horse and carts were very much the order of the day.

63

the responsibilities of Highways very much in my mind I wrote to the Area Surveyor. There was no relaxing of attitude, but a site meeting was arranged with one of his assistants. We were to survey the length of Downdale Road and look at the proposed locations.

I was not too happy about two of them. At this point I was quite prepared to discuss the passing places, but my strategy was then to question the degree (if any) of my responsibility to improve this road. The man in question was again very amicable and he agreed, that the proposals, in their present form would be difficult. He not only agreed to changes but made some useful suggestions. Now it was up to me. I had to get an architect to draw plans of the sections of road involved with details of each passing place. I had then to submit them for approval before work could commence.

I had still not signed the agreement and my attitude was getting less favourable.

Costs and more costs. Oh and I almost forgot, we had to pay for, and erect passing place signs.

Again I wrote the Surveyor. 'There are seven farms, several private houses, holiday cottages, a camping and caravan site and an engineering workshop all generating traffic. It is grossly unfair and unreasonable to expect me to pay for the whole of these road improvements.' At 10,000 visitors a year, in one week that was approximately 150 cars or only 6 cars an hour. Less sometimes than local traffic volume. He was unmoved. 'I shall be obliged to refer you back to the Planning Officer' was his only comment.

I tried endless times — even quoting a letter from a previous visit by a Planning Officer less than three years earlier when he had stated he had consulted Highways and they (at that time) had no objections to this development providing facilities were provided to turn vehicles, off the road. Again he was not impressed, 'Those were only off the cuff comments.'

I decided what we needed was a questionnaire in the form of a visitor's own survey of the access, and any problems they had encountered. We carried it out on 1,000 visitors over a peak period commencing Spring Bank Holiday 1990. (See Appendix II)

The results were enlightening. We asked three questions as follows:
1. Did you meet any other vehicle travelling in the opposite direction on your journey down the lane? (Downdale Road)
2. Did you have any problem or passing difficulty with any other vehicle on Downdale Road.

3.   In view of the narrow and winding access road do you think the enterprise worthwhile and should it be encouraged?

A space was left headed 'Comments.'

Visitors were invited to answer the questions honestly and of their own free will.

The results were as follows.

817 recorded no problems and out of these

465 made mostly very favourable comments.

26 recorded no problems but suggested minor improvements to the road, by the Local Authority. 42 had managed to misinterpret the questions and only

10 had any problem at all and again most only minor.

The rest were either taken away or picked up by children for recreational use!

The reason I am putting these facts together is to demonstrate the effort and hard work that went into our campaign.

It was not just about showmanship or bellicosity, it was about calculated research and a sound defence.   Obviously the Shire Horse incident at Helmsley had highlighted what I considered to be heavy handed dictatorial action.

I have to say that the results of our survey are verifiable and now rest with Yorkshire and Humberside Tourist Board at York. They have subsequently been used for student research.

As commercial members of the board it is worth recording the excellent support we received from the Development Manager at that time. Also from the Director of Tourism and Amenities for Scarborough Borough Council.

The affair rumbled on and in an effort to enlighten the local population and other interested parties, Staintondale Parish Council called a public meeting at the Village Hall at 7.30 June 20th, 1990.

A Planning Officer and members of North Yorkshire County Council were present.

It could be described as a non event, with few pertinent questions and a lot of outright curiosity. One question stuck in my mind, or my throat! 'When were the passing places going to be provided?' Spoken quite loftily.

'Just as soon as Mr. Jenkins signs the agreement' came the reply.

Nobody thought to mention that the agreement had only just been sent to me. An agreement ensuing from the retrospective planning application in January!

CHAPTER TWELVE
THE NUTCRACKERS

This was the all important meeting. The planners were going to recommend that the retrospective application be refused and that the County Secretary be authorised to commence enforcement proceedings against us. In other words, after all the effort and negotiations they were still prepared to close me down.

It was October 10th 1990 at the Parks headquarters, Helmsley. By now I was an old hand at facing such threats and I had already acquired an agenda from County Hall. The notes about the background were still unchanged. They were misleading and inaccurate. This time I decided to take action.

Another paragraph headed 'Conclusion' also caught my eye. It stated that I found the Committee's requirements 'unreasonable and unacceptable.' This was nonsense and taken totally out of context. On the contrary I had found quite a few Councillors sympathetic and some very supportive and helpful.

What these remarks had been aimed at was the road improvements in the shape of passing places on Downdale Road.

I accepted that there was a degree of responsibility but how much was a degree?

You will have gathered from my last paragraph that I was less than happy about the whole affair. I was also worried about the cost. Again I wrote to all Councillors on the development control sub-committee prior to the meeting. (See Appendix I)

My objections to certain conditions were carefully set out, and I explained my reasons for them. I also set out a projected cost, and also the job losses that would result if I was closed down. My opinion at the meeting was that the 'Conclusion' 2.4 paragraph had got to them first! Well a possibility. I sat and listened to the planners presentation with critical interest.

It was mainly about the discussions, but I did notice a slight shift of emphasis on the passing places. Paragraph 2.5 (extract) 'was aware, that such passing places were likely to be required.' Generally though it was a fair assessment, and my co-operation and help towards trying to reach agreements on other issues was mentioned. But, now the big but! 'Mr. Jenkins will only sign an agreement he thinks fair and reasonable. He considers that the road carries an ever increasing amount of local traffic with increasingly large agricultural vehicles and considers he should only therefore have to pay for two out of the four passing places.'

'Hear, hear!' I felt like shouting, but of course you are not allowed to speak.

I waited anxiously for a response from the floor. What about my impassioned plea. Did nobody share my viewpoint? Had anybody even read my letter. Would the enforcement action be pursued? One Councillor stood up. 'Mr. Chairman', he said 'Don't you think that we are taking a sledgehammer to crack a nut? Surely if Mr. Jenkins is prepared to pay for two passing places and his budget is stretched, can we not ask him to pay for the other two spaced over the next couple of years?'

In the meantime another Councillor had made a late entry, and had glanced at what I assumed was my letter. I am not going to quote what he said because I am sure it was meant as a light-hearted remark. But I got the impression it implied that this planning applicant was a Nut that should be cracked. He then went on 'The four thousand pounds that Mr. Jenkins is saying that he is committed to, is only a bond — a surety. He doesn't have to pay it at this moment in time.'

Well at least my letter had been read. In it I had listed the cost of these conditions and what I already had spent on a new road. With the fencing, tree planting and landscaping, plus the passing places, it ran into thousands of pounds. I didn't believe my small enterprise could stand it. At 10,000 visitors a season it was nothing. Less than the weekly intake at some major attractions.

There was a slight lull in proceedings. I think the next question was on several Councillor's lips and waiting to be asked.

'Could we have the last amount explained' said someone. 'And how a figure of four thousand pounds was arrived at?'

Everybody was looking towards the Planning Officer. The Planning Officer was looking towards the County Secretary. 'Could you explain to the meeting?'

There was at this point, just a hint of conferring between official heads, seemingly in agreement. 'Well', said the Secretary 'It appears that this is the estimated cost of four passing places, and the amount referred to, is the amount Mr. Jenkins would have to pay if for one reason or another he couldn't or didn't carry out the work. In other words 'in default' of the agreement. The County Council would then do them and Mr. Jenkins would pay the bond to cover the cost!

I couldn't believe my ears. Knowing glances were exchanged between various people. My estimate in my letter to the Councillors had been more than double that. In fact if any problems had been encountered with the main services I had referred to, or unstable embankments, just one of them could have cost the amount they were talking about.

Leaning over to my wife, I whispered, 'At that price let them carry out the work. Come on let's go home and put a cheque in the post today.'

In the meantime the meeting had decided to accept the proposal put forward by the first motion. We were followed outside by eager reporters and two Councillors.

I reaffirmed my next move 'It's a cheque in the post today, the dispute is over.'

One of the Councillors spoke 'And don't delay — do it. We don't want you bringing anything back here!' The other one laughed. There was relief and hugs all round. It had been an eighteen month struggle and at times an ordeal.

The reporters closed in looking for the report in tomorrow's newspapers.

The jubilation was evident, the relief rather more personal.

Next day it was 'Victory for Shire Horse Farm' and 'A Jubilant Tony Jenkins etc etc.'

It brought telephone calls, letters and cards from many people.

I owe a debt of gratitude to a lot of special people not least my planning adviser, courtesy of R.D.C. There are many, many more, it would not be courteous to mention just some of the names or of various associations but thanks to you all.

It seemed our personal traumas were at an end. In November 1990 we received our green coloured planning approval certificate, and for a few days the relief was indescribable.

There was more trouble waiting in the wings. Just a few more

Victory for Shire Horse Farm.

days after celebrating our success, two ominous looking envelopes arrived in our post box.

Two County Court summons — one for each of us. Do you remember the irrelevant solicitor's letter earlier in the book?

This was not the end of our problems, it was only the end of the beginning.

It is now nearing the end of 1993 and litigation still continues.

Well Kipling, I am still filling the unforgiving minute (again with apologies) and hopefully my sixty seconds of distance run, will give me some reward.

I consider that I shall have earned it!. If I allowed this book to end on anything other than a happy note, I should have failed in my belief in old fashioned values.

In spite of our personal distress at what we consider to be, totally unjustified legal action, a silver lining emerged from the darker clouds. In July 1993 for our contribution towards (would you believe?) successfully integrating Tourism with the Environment, we won a Yorkshire and Humberside Tourist Board 'White Rose Award.'

More than that, we were also nominated by an independent panel for 'England for Excellence.' The ultimate accolade we still strive for.

CHAPTER THIRTEEN
HAD WE SHOT A ROBIN?

In the closing lines of the previous chapter I referred to the end of the beginning. The beginning of the end was to be as elusive as the peace of mind that we hoped would accompany our eventual victory.

The irrelevant letter of January 1990 followed by the summons in November of that year was the prelude to over three years of distress and trauma. A law suit brought about for no apparent reason but one that was to cost us dearly.

The plaintiff's case was supported by a legal aid certificate. It was also made much worse by the fact that they were also close neighbours and had been personal friends for over twenty years.

Other elements were now to add to our problems. In December a terrible storm blew up which woke us in the early hours. The wind was screaming and every timber beam and rafter shook and shuddered. Outside heavy bangs and thumps interspersed with the sounds of wind blown objects being dispatched with a force that was frightening filled the air. I peered out of the windows in to a black night. It sounded as if the whole farm was being ripped apart. What hand of darkness was this? The cold grey dawn slowly made its presence felt. Sleep had been impossible so I had sat there just waiting while my imagination ran riot.

I tried to reassure myself that it was probably not as bad as it sounded but I really did fear the worst. The wind was still screaming and inside this old house with its two foot thick walls it seemed a haven. I felt very grateful for that. Outside it was very different. Wild was an understatement. I slowly got dressed and mentally urged the daylight on. Were the horses safe, had they been hit by some of the flying debris? Had we any pantiles left on and what other devastating damage had occurred and how much more was to come? We could only wait and see. With plenty of weather protection zipped and buttoned I took the handlamp and ventured forth. In the shelter of the farm courtyard it didn't seem too bad because the wind was pretty well a straight Northerly.

Once away from this shelter and as daylight slowly filtered through the dark I was suddenly caught up in what seemed like a whirlwind. Metal sheets were flapping on building roofs and the sound of tearing timber and crashing structures filled the air. It sounded like something from a hurricane scene in a film.

I suddenly thought about the rabbits of all things, they were all housed in the pets corner which was sited in the large open fronted barn which also accommodates all our carts and waggons.

Hanging on to my hat and struggling to keep my feet I set off down the track. I hadn't gone far before some of the devastated scene began to unfold. Pieces of corrugated Perspex sheet were blowing everywhere and all around me as darkness gave way to dawn, I could see broken pantiles, torn off guttering and debris, everywhere. What a mess.

The wind was relentless as I passed the barn where we keep the Thresher. All the roof lights had been ripped out and litter was scattered everywhere. Worse was to come. I turned into the paddock and realised just how bad things were. The wind was being tunnelled through the natural cutting linking us to Rigg Hall and coming straight in off the North Sea. It had struck a corner of what we were still calling the new building and smashed into it with all the force of a typhoon.

The scene which now met my eyes was one of total devastation. There was no respite either. Eighteen foot lengths of corrugated steel sheets were being torn off the roof and sent flying through the air like a pack of playing cards. I watched in horror — we had ten horses living out in the surrounding fields and these sheets could have sliced into a horse with the ease of a butcher's cleaver.

They were taking off and landing way out of sight into the gloomy daybreak. Gloomy was the situation. What did I say about my sinking heart?

I remembered the purpose of my mission — The Rabbits.

Now I really did have a problem, the risk to life and limbs was now graphically apparent. The section of roof immediately over the rabbits had gone, and more was under threat. I made my way round to this area keeping in the shelter of the hay barn. This was the epicentre of this destructive storm. Fortunately the hay barn was full of hay so it was well ballasted and secure. Once round this I was staring into the full force of the gale.

Across the back of the pets corner two horizontal 7" x 2" baulks of timber with vertical steel cladding were bending like an archer's bow. Any minute it looked like something was about to give. In front of this corner section, still on their respective benches stood a variety of rabbit hutches with their residents inside. The only thing to do was to wait for a lull in the wind, rush in and grab a hutch and run like the clappers well something like that.

I stood poised — here we go — number one! It was like some kind of crazy relay race but this was not a game. Seven times I made this mercy dash and seven times later the rabbits were safely housed within the shelter of the next door hay barn. By now of course there was plenty of light and I could see the full extent and radius of the damage.

The roofing sheets were distributed over five fields some struck vertically in the ground, I shuddered. Better go and check the horses. With great difficulty I started along the track. One eye out for flying object and one for a sighting of the horses. I now knew what our friends in America suffered at the hands of a Tornado and this was just a cyclonic wind. Just!

The wind was hostile and frenzied and I was well aware of my predicament. At the time although I was not to know, it had taken the slate roof off Rigg Hall just one hundred and fifty yards to the North of us. My son, daughter in law and children were virtually prisoners. Trapped inside by flying roof tiles!

I found my way to a point where the underground culvert across the gravelled car park area runs into the ditch. A corrugated roofing sheet was buried deep into the hedgebank it had severed every stem and basal shoot at ground level and left a gaping hole.

The wind behind me now, I carried on down the track. Roofing nails and washers were strewn everywhere and shattered pieces of perspex roof light glistened in the grass verges. What a cleanup operation was in store. By now I could see clearly across the fields and what a sight met my eyes. Roofing sheets smashed, purlins and timber lay everywhere. It had blown far beyond our boundary and into the field where our original access crossed.

My assistant didn't arrive until 9am. What a shock she would get. I was down as far as Mascot's field now and the horses had seen me. Mascot came flying down his field, hooves kicking up great divots of mud. The wind stirs horses up and seems to make them nervous. Today was no exception and it was still with ecstatic relief that I watched them rearing and plunging with no visible signs of injury. Wonderful. I think they did their equivalent of a war dance just to let me know all was well. As I glanced along what had been a newly constructed stock wire fence, I could see a section that had been severed by a wind born flying missile in the form of a steel roofing sheet.

Slowly I returned to the farm. Although the horses were safe I must admit that I felt pretty miserable. This was the destruction of my pride and joy, our lovely new open fronted pole barn. So much admired and so useful on wet days to entertain our visitors. I consoled myself at least it was insured.

The salvage operation was both hard and arduous. These eighteen foot sheets were heavy and in their buckled state unwieldy. Shattered and splintered timber, endless amounts of nails and washers, debris of all sorts. It all had to be cleared.

I should add that this building was nearly a hundred foot long and thirty three-feet wide. There was a lot of roof! Armed with a petrol driven Stihl saw and a large trailer we set about it. Sheets had to be cut for transportation and whole sections of roof dismantled. It took us several days. There was an extensive insurance claim form to complete and some immediate roof repairs to be carried out. These applied to the small range of stone buildings on the yard. We were given the go ahead on these.

I was told to get estimates for the larger roof previously described, but that didn't present any real problems. Well, not until we submitted them that is.

You will all have heard of small print. To cut a long and, complicated story short it led to a visit by a firm of loss adjusters. It seems their job is to see that the insurance company pays out as little as possible and that you don't have as much of the insurance protection wrapped round you as you thought you had! 'Well Mr J. it seems, judging from the roof estimates that your building was under insured' the voice of you know who.

'That's ridiculous, I insured the building only two years ago for a sum agreed with the company'.

'Ah but inflation'.

'I don't know about inflation', I felt like exploding. I followed up:'If the company had made any suggestion at renewal time I would have listened. The house is index linked why not a similar scheme on farm buildings?'

'On a self build scheme using part reclaimed materials actual replacement value is sometimes difficult'. He said that he would see what he could do and make a written offer. I knew I was saying goodbye to watching roofing contractors put a new roof on. Another large D.I.Y. kit in the shape of Tony Jenkins and his able assistant loomed large. Never mind we did it, and it looked none the worse. We had a few hairy moments though. Once when we were up on this roof in some sort of force eight wind, the ladder blew down. We were stranded on the roof.

Before the roof had been reinstated as it were, another body blow struck. Severe weather and snow in February 1991 brought even more problems. What a sad and miserable sight it made. A building stripped of its roof hung in tatters and its once proud contents were now exposed to the pitiless elements.

My lovely restored vehicles looked lost and forlorn. I wanted to rush in, clean off the snow and wet and take them into the house. The way a child would gather up its toys. Kipling, my adopted mentor had a line to suit my predicament, 'If you can see the things you gave your life to broken'.

A bit melodramatic even for me I suppose, but it suited the situation. This period was probably the most traumatic of our lives. It had included a Christmas when we should have been celebrating our planning victory and instead we were beginning to feel like outcasts. The summons had prompted a telephone call to County Hall. After all the claim for trespass and damage had been motivated by the planning conditions imposed upon us. We were advised to see a Solicitor.

Don't ever get involved in legal litigation. It is a minefield. We were to discover the complexities and its pitfalls to our cost.

Only one local man inspired me to keep my head above water that, Christmas. Unfortunately he has now prematurely passed away. He was a former Rugby playing colleague who worked for the Duchy of Lancaster. I had gone down to get our Christmas tree. 'Roy' I said 'you have restored my faith in human nature'.

At the onset we were warned of the serious disadvantages of fighting a legal aided claim. We were never going to win.

Just about coincident with the Winter storms another shot across the bows was delivered. A second letter from the same source of solicitor, this time with what was later described at trial as a ransom demand. It was for a host of miscellaneous demands but not least for five thousand pounds and their costs. I saw it as frivolous and unjustified. It wasn't some kind of nightmare was it? We had bought the land now being used for the new access road in good faith from our neighbours and now it seemed they were either going to stop us using it or hold us to ransom. It posed another serious threat of closure and once more we had to fight.

CHAPTER FOURTEEN
WE RAISE THE WORLD'S WATER TABLE

Those of you who had read my first book will remember a chapter called 'Cool Clear Water' and a line that read 'Have you left a tap turned on outside?'

Nobody could have imagined that this same question would be asked again several years on. It was! At about 10pm on Tuesday, 13th August, 1991. Ann was just about to make a cup of tea. It had been a lovely sunny day and an extremely busy one at that. She turned on the tap — no water!

'Have you left a tap on outside?' I couldn't believe my ears. Shot a robin, I think we must have run over a black cat as well.

'Well I suppose it's possible', I said. I knew the girls had been filling water troughs.

Again I grabbed a handlamp and went out to do the rounds. There hadn't been any indication of the spring slowing down so I was a little bit optimistic. I should explain to other readers that this farm is served by a spring supply — we have no mains water.

I checked all outside taps and troughs and then climbed up into the loft. My optimism was misguided. There were no taps on but equally there was no water. The tanks were empty.

It was now the proverbial trudge up the field, a several hundred yard trek in the dark using the lamp. As I approached the site of the storage tanks I stopped to listen. It is possible under normal circumstances to hear the sound of water trickling in. All was silent. With untypical pessimism I screwed off the plastic manhole cover and shone the lamp inside the tank. It was empty.

Tomorrow was the peak day of our season and we could not open without water. No sleep tonight either and that was also a fact.

It is not until you have experienced a situation that you actually realise the implications. This applies particularly to water. Imagine a good old fashioned hot summer's day and twelve thirsty horses for starters. Add to that a hundred plus visitors all wanting a cup of tea — and worse, wanting to use the loo!

Well suffice to say we had to get some and as soon as possible. Just as soon as I got back in the house I grabbed the telephone. I knew a man who might have some ideas — his name was John Brand.

Luckily for me a rescue plan was put together. It involved two local firms who between them worked wonders. Our next big problem was stopping visitors making the journey down the lane and not deterring them from returning the following day. I put together a desperate message and made a big sign 'Closed Today for Emergency Repairs'. That same morning a 3,000 gallon tanker and tractor unit belonging to Ray Owen wound its way down our lane and made its way slowly and cautiously across our fields — well over twenty tons in total. We need not have worried, the ground was rock hard. A succession of dry summers and the lack of snow and heavy rain had stripped the land of moisture and the water table was at an all time low. Even the old stoned hedgebanks were collapsing as the soil turned to dust.

1991 generally hadn't been a bad year for us so far as visitors were concerned. I think the press and television publicity over the planning dispute had certainly boosted interest in our enterprise. In addition of course, the ending of the gulf war had brought more business from people who would otherwise have been abroad. The last thing we wanted was a crisis such as a water problem.

Our spring was still rising but slowly, so each day a trek up the field to top up the storage tanks from the tanker. At this moment in time the legal dispute was taking a back seat but was ominously still there. Other more pressing problems and thoughts filled my mind. What if the spring failure was permanent and what if the hole in the ozone layer was causing the problem — worse, suppose we didn't get much snow again this winter? We could not run a business or indeed much else without water and the nearest mains water was over a mile away. A mile as the crow flies but on the other side of what now appeared to be hostile territory. It might just as well have been a million miles. I shrugged it off, it didn't bear thinking about.

August ran into September quite quickly and soon the demand on our water supply started to subside. This was only due to the gradual decrease in visitor numbers. The weather had been excellent warm, sunny and very pleasant.

On Tuesday 3rd September we attended a ceremony at Rudding Park to receive our commendation in the Yorkshire and Humberside Tourist Board White Rose Awards. Proof that rather than being detrimental to the environment we had shown that it was possible successfully to integrate one with the other! This was something that I intended to pursue with relish.

Well at least some good news and justifiable celebration. We had a wonderful and enthusiastic staff and the award was well deserved. The season ended on a sunny day on September 26th. There had been no rain for two months.

In spite of all the problems, 1991 had been an eventful year and the Tourism and Environment Award had opened up new horizons. Plans had been laid for a whole farm conservation scheme which was both idealistic and ambitious. From my own point of view it was going to be the realisation of a dream. Reality in the meantime struck back. We received a letter from our Solicitor to say that a site meeting had been arranged with the other side for Monday December 9th. It turned out to be something of a non event and the vagueness of both legal representatives struck me forcibly.

One question by the opposition's man infuriated me 'Has there been a recent search made on the status of this lane?' I was blazing. This from people who had taken out a summons and accepted legal aid on the strength of supposedly sound facts and substantial evidence. Quietly and to myself I determined to approach the plaintiffs personally after this meeting and show them our conveyance deed and copies of recent searches which we had in our possession. I still did not believe they even had a case.

It was not an easy thing for me to do when the time came but I steeled myself. After all we had been close friends and any effort to salvage something was well worthwhile.

I carefully prepared the relevant documents which their solicitor had requested sight of. Our neighbours were to have a preview. I telephoned first and explained my proposal which was to try and convince them that we had acted in good faith and that the County Council had authorised the roadworks insisting that the road was a public highway. It was a claim that according to our conveyance was indisputable.

Our neighbours were receptive and willing to see the documents. I took them round. It was December and Christmas was looming large. I couldn't think of a better time to try for some reconciliation.

They seemed quite relieved that at least I was trying to sort things out and listened carefully to all I had to say. It was made clear that my visit was without prejudice and only an attempt to give them a clear picture of the situation and the events leading up to it. The documents I explained in detail and one in particular that was a copy of a search to the local authority made by their Solicitor for a transaction for themselves. It clearly stated that the road was a public highway maintainable at public expense.

At the end of this in depth discussion it was agreed that the dispute must end. We were both to make immediate contact with our solicitors and tell them a solution must be found. I walked on air as I got into my car. It was a wonderful feeling and I couldn't wait to get home to tell my wife. Christmas would be Christmas this year and my parting comment to our neighbours was that it was wonderful to be talking again. I meant it.

That Christmas we had decided to hold a couple of Sunday Open Days which we described as an experience of an old fashioned Christmas. They were to be in aid of Scarborough branch of Save the Children. They were an amazing success. Members of the branch volunteered to help and a plan was carefully prepared. It included a very lifelike nativity scene set in the stables using full size models and a beautifully decorated coffee shop and a huge Christmas tree.

The old Edwardian wall post box could be used for letters to Santa and I was to be the man himself. We had a full outfit complete with beard and a few Yo, oh ohs would complete the picture.

Christmas carols were a must so I also elected to strum these on my guitar and lead the carols. It was an unmitigated success and the children loved it. You can imagine the picture — lots of happy smiling children sat round a beautifully decorated Christmas tree singing carols with Santa. Wonderful.

Christmas fare was on offer, Turkey Soup and Sandwiches, Mince Pies with Brandy Butter, Christmas Cake and Hot Chestnuts. A real old fashioned Christmas.

We have a lovely old but restored horse drawn sleigh and in the absence of reindeer (oh dear, no deer, no), we stood two Shetland ponies in front and loaded it with Christmas parcels. It was a truly marvellous event and one that was to be repeated. More than that I was happy doing it. My heart was lighter and hopefully it would remain that way. I was to send a very important letter to my solicitor and I couldn't wait. This particular Christmas brought even more glad tidings. It brought a visit from John Taylor, an old neighbour who just happened to be in the water bore hole business — we were about to raise the world's water table!

CHAPTER FIFTEEN
A YEAR OF MANY MANTLES

There is one striking feature about this farm and that has been its progressive and varied projects. Every year I find myself dreaming up some new scheme or additional facility and not least of these was the rebuilding and cladding of the old pole hay barn. Wet and cold weather was a problem and we had to have a covered area to get visitors inside. I had decided a studio type room with a small stage and seating would serve a dual purpose. It could be used as an educational facility and a video projection studio. We could show our own videos or possibly purchase a suitable one to use. I could also use my big screen and slide projector for talks of my own.

As usual a trip to a reclaimed timber yard came first. The materials are sound, available and reasonably priced. I drew up a plan for the conversion and carefully took off the quantity of materials. It was a lorry load.

We had just got this lot off loaded and neatly stacked and sheeted when I had a visitor — our local insurance manager. He was at the farm to re-schedule the farm buildings and contents insurance. Another way of saying higher premiums. It was amazing really because after the round of inspection he came in the house for a chat.

'I don't honestly think that the company will be too happy keeping cover on that old hay barn out there.' He looked towards me for comment.

I grinned, 'Fear not', I said 'That great pile of timber under the blue plastic sheet, is for exactly that purpose. We are going fully to renovate it'. I explained exactly what I had in mind and a little gleam seemed to shine from his gaze. 'Better come and have a look when it's done. You will obviously need increased and extended cover on something like that.'

Running parallel with this, the plan was being prepared for our whole farm conservation project. Something that seemed almost daunting in its magnitude but so worthy and important to me and this property. I determined that we should go for it. The work was to include creating a wildlife pond, regenerating all the ancient hedgerows, and planting yards and yards of new ones, planting a small broadleaved amenity woodland and rebuilding what seemed like miles of drystone walling. What a wonderful achievement to aim for. As you can imagine my mind and hands were full. Never a dull moment. I think all these things kept me so occupied that I managed to push the legal dispute to the back of my mind but it wasn't going to stay there. I think I was of the opinion that no news is good news. I actually thought that my visit to our neighbours was possibly leading towards a settlement. Perhaps they had decided to drop the proceedings. Alas my hopes and dreams were shattered. On the 25th March 1992 we received a letter from our Solicitor. It said that in spite of the deeds and documents which included the searches, that the opposition had seen and copied, they were still pressuring us to proceed towards trial.

So much for my December visit and Christmas goodwill. Well it wasn't Christmas now and my feelings about goodwill to all men had gone with the tinsel and melted with the snow. Our solicitors were still pointing to the legal aid certificate that our neighbours had secured and warning me of the dire consequences of not trying to reach a settlement. Apparently I was effectively in a 'no win' situation.

Well with apologies to Rudyard Kipling again, this is the bit when you do make a heap of all your winnings and risk it on one turn of pitch and toss. I would fight this injustice if it cost me every penny. Blackmail I would not tolerate and being held to ransom is something I did not intend living with. Needless to say I wrote a very very strong letter back.

For a bit of light relief let us return to the divine experience of drilling a bore hole! If I said that my very good friend and previous neighbour John was a wild version lookalike and larger-than-life David Bellamy then I wouldn't be far wrong. You, the reader would have a very good mental picture of this wonderful man and we can all enjoy sharing the experience.

If you remember seeing pictures of nuclear missiles and their mobile launching platforms, that is what this rig looked like as it crossed the field along what I have previously referred to as the stripe. On the tracked prime mover, pipe in mouth and laughing all over his face sat the man himself. His effortless and casual precision amazed me — he could have been driving a garden tractor. 'Hi Jenki' he yelled above the roar of this massive diesel compressor, 'I'll just take her through the gate and on to the lane'. I watched in amazement. He steered this complicated contraption of goodness knows what length through a ten foot gate opening with less than inches to spare. That was only the arrival of the machine. The events that followed are very worthy of a story.

This man knew his job. He was here as a mate and a friend and I had every confidence in his ability. He walked into our orchard and found spaces between trees. Looking at me he said 'Where's your septic tank and soil pipe?' I nodded towards the house 'Down across there', I said, pointing. He looked down at the ground between his feet, 'Right, we will go down here.'

This decision, made without the slightest hesitation heralded the start of a very rewarding experience and in more ways than one. You can go without food for days on end but you cannot survive many without water. At that time our very future depended on it.

The machine and its rig now had to be manoeuvred through the gate into the orchard and the drill and gantry erected. I was fascinated and intrigued. John joked, 'How far above sea level are you?' Realising immediately what he meant I said 'Three hundred foot so make sure you strike water before that depth — we can get salt-water from the sea!'

Now we watched as the whole rig was assembled. What a sight to behold and what an unlikely structure to be standing so loftily among the apple and pear trees. John spoke again 'There'll be a lot of muck you know — dust'll be everywhere. It will cover these trees and t'house as well I wouldn't wonder'.

This was something I hadn't thought about but I didn't have long to wait to see his words come true. The first fifty feet or so wasn't too bad, soft going in fact and I was told that this was unusually deep for unstable ground. It would need casing. Then we hit the rock. "That's better" said this curly haired and bearded figure, 'We need to get into rock'. By now the dust was rising in clouds and the green leaves and blossom of the fruit trees began to turn white. This was only the start, we had a long way to go.

You have got to picture the scene at this point. It was priceless.

This heavy mantle of stone dust was descending at a rate of knots. The curly hair and beard were also by now white with it. His shirt almost unbuttoned to the waist was full of it. It hung over his belt like a pack horse's carrier bags. In his mouth stuck his pipe and the bowl was full of it. Even the pocket in his shirt hung forward full to overflowing. He stood there at the controls of this powerful throbbing machinery completely oblivious and totally engrossed in his quest for water. He

You have got to picture the scene at this point.

looked as if he would be the first to need it. He was watching closely the spoil being thrown up by the drill. Suddenly he reached down and picked up a handful. 'That's better Jenki — water bearing gravel — we are getting there'.

He said we were down about a hundred feet and by now I was getting excited. It was a truly wonderful experience. Suddenly we saw the gravel getting wetter and the excitement was exhilarating. 'Will there be a gusher' I said 'Well I'll soon make you one' came the reply. 'We blow compressed air down and the water comes up — and we shall soon be able to do it'. I couldn't wait. When the water started to emerge it was pure ecstasy. I could hardly believe it. At this point I had to leave the proceedings to attend to other things.

Only a few minutes later the mobile phone rang and our intrepid diviner had left the rig to answer it. I could see he looked thoughtful as he left his van so I called over, 'Everything all right?' It was not the answer I wanted. 'Not exactly' he said, 'We've lost the water. Come and have a listen it just sounds like somebody's pulled out the bath plug!'

I was knocked for six and I think it showed. 'Oh heck, that's terrible. What do we do?' There was not a moment's hesitation in his reply. With typical and supreme optimism bordering on the casual, he simply said, 'Don't worry we'll catch up with it again — just go deeper'. I found his manner very reassuring. He knew his job and I was quite happy to take his word.

At something over one hundred and fifty feet we struck again and this time for real. We could hear from the surface the magic sound of babbling running water.

'There's two underground streams down there Jenki. One running into the other and enough to push up a gusher. Go and get your camera'.

What a moment, this time I couldn't hide my excitement or my pleasure. I thought I would explode. These are life's incredible experiences and must be recorded. This was the ultimate in cool, clear water, and at this depth its purity was a forgone conclusion.

We leave this happy situation to pick up the parallel because we have got to return to the conservation plan. Part of this plan was the creation of a wildlife pond, and the difficulty now facing us was the fact that it was intended to be filled with the original farm spring overflow. Alas it was no longer overflowing.

Well the plan must go ahead and my mind was filled with a remark I had heard about two moorland farmers who had built a sheep dip. One had said to the other 'What are we going to fill it with?' The other had replied 'God'll fill it!' Well I felt about the same but I couldn't help some serious reservations. I couldn't think of a worse sight than an empty basin of earth just growing weeds. We had started the pond excavation just after we closed in September of that year. It was ideal dry conditions for the work of a 4 WD J.C.B. excavator but not ideal for the time when we needed to fill it. I had estimated at least eighty thousand gallons.

You are hardly going to believe this next bit. In October we decided to take a short break at the Manor House at Ingleby Greenhow in a self catering apartment. It was about thirty miles to the north of us. On the second morning of our visit, Ann called me to the bedroom window. 'Just come and look out here'.

I almost said, 'Do I need to?' I was enjoying a no-work-today-slow-to-gain-consciousness morning. I suspected it must be a peacock on the lawn or some other exotic species. With reluctance I dragged myself out of bed and across to the window. I blinked, blinked again and pinched myself. Our car, other cars, the lawn and the courtyard were white over with snow! And it was still coming down like goosefeathers. 'I can't believe this', I said to Ann, 'Just can't believe it.

What a week to choose for a holiday. It snowed, it rained, it sleeted and then it rained again. Heavy, incessant, persistent and wet!! Field corners were flooded, stretches of road stood in water and everywhere was soaked. I looked upwards, 'Well good job it's a pond and not just a sheep-dip!'

We drove home that Saturday, most of the route over the North York Moors. When at last we started to drop down towards Ravenscar the full effect of the rain was evident all the way. Water stood in huge puddles by roadside and low lying areas of fields were flooded.

We eventually turned off the A171 and headed for our destination. Again I could hardly wait. As we drove along towards the Shepherds Arms I looked towards the coast. There was a pond in nearly every field.

There is a name for this particular law when you have just sunk a borehole but I wasn't complaining. We arrived home to find our pond happily completed and its overflow discharging water in the ditch at an estimated several thousand gallons an hour. Had it not been for the flood overspill the pressure would have washed the banks away. Ah well, the water table was very low!

CHAPTER SIXTEEN
PERGE SED CAUTE

A Spring conference of North Yorkshire Farming and Wildlife advisers group led me to a chance meeting with Doctor Malcolm Bell a man whose forthright manner and single mindedness I had long admired. He was associate adviser with a law firm recognised by FWAG. Was this the opportunity I had been waiting for? Could he advise me on what positive steps I might take to dent the confidence of the opposition and what exactly did he think of such a situation? It was after all a result of planning conditions imposed upon us and why should we be burdened with such crippling costs.

After the meeting which was held here on 30th March 1993 I had a quiet word. 'Well yes, certainly I could look at the background and some of the documents. From what you have told me it seems grossly unfair that you should have to capitulate just because of a legal aid certificate. Leave it with me a few days and I will contact you.'

He was as good as his word and in April an appointment was made for us to visit his office and together with a legal adviser they would give us their frank opinion.

We were not disappointed. After a lengthy discussion and examination of a massive file of documents which we had in our possession it was decided that we should get copies of certain documents from our own solicitors. I

The Jenkins family motto — 'Go on but cautiously'.

in my innocence could see nothing wrong in this. After all they were pushing me to settle on economic grounds and I was looking for an economic fight. Who could convince me of the best solution?

I have got to say at this point that the Jenkins family motto is *'Perge sed caute'* meaning 'Go on but cautiously'.

Well I wanted to bear this in mind but on the other hand the family crest is a battle axe! Without going into details I have got to record that seeking advice elsewhere did not suit everybody and we soon found ourselves transferring the brief. Understandable I suppose but I wanted advice that I wanted to hear. After all it was me that had to live with my conscience when I had sacrificed my principles.

At this point further counsel advice was sought and how very reassuring and stimulating it turned out to be. "Of course there is a risk of losing. In legal matters there always is, but you have all the evidence and supportive documents in your favour. It is a mercenary affair and without the support of legal aid it would not have been pursued." He recommended that a second application be made to the legal aid board without delay. The certificate in his opinion should be discharged.

I must mention here in fairness that upon my own insistence, our previous solicitor had made a similar request. They in fact put together an excellent written submission which was rejected.

The same position was upheld. It was now a collision course with destiny. Expert evidence would possibly be needed and witnesses would be vital. I took this very seriously. No stone had to be left unturned and anything that could give a clear picture including maps and photographs would be help. I decided to start with Highways at County Hall. The definitive map. A booklet entitled 'Rights of Way Act 1990' had specifically stated that the routes shown on this map were absolute and final. They were legal and binding. I took my assistant with me and I asked to see it. The clerk was very helpful and to our delight it showed everything we wanted to know. More than that we were given a copy of the road schedule in Staintondale which was conclusive. We came back in high spirits — one to us anyway!

I do not intend to bore anybody to death by quoting blow by blow details of the period leading up to the trial. Our counsel had prepared a request for further and better particulars of the Plaintiff's claim and some interrogatories. He felt it was important to pin down the detail of this claim.

Our solicitor pursuing Counsel advice had pointed out to the legal aid board in the one last try to get the Plaintiff's legal aid certificates discharged, that this was a cynical and pointless piece of litigation which nobody in his right mind who was paying his own costs would contemplate.

He had not held out much hope in this direction and so the rejection I mentioned earlier came as no surprise. We had of course made a final plea to the plaintiff's solicitor to consult again with his clients, who of course were still our neighbours, and see if they were prepared to consider a reasonable settlement. It brought nothing more than a rebuff in that they were still seeking five thousand pounds to settle the case plus their costs. They also said it was a pity that we hadn't paid this amount earlier when their costs would have been lower.

I mentally thought about the family motto, 'Go on but cautiously' and decided to throw the caution bit to the wind. A settlement now was out of the question and a battle axe seemed a very appropriate symbol.

The rest of the Summer of 1993 was tempered by the pleasure we had all shared in preparing for and winning the Yorkshire and Humberside White Rose award for Tourism and the Environment. Our wonderful and enthusiastic staff worked so very hard and deserved a large share of the credit.

This farm in itself is idyllic. It is set in beautiful countryside on the North York Moors National Park coastline. It is south facing and set in a mass of summer colour and foliage.

We could never hope to compete with what nature had provided but with our carefully planned conservation work we had certainly enhanced a beautiful situation.

In November we flew to New Zealand and I seriously believe had we not done so, one or both of us would have cracked under the strain. Once our season ended in September it became impossible not to eat, sleep and think anything other than the impending court case. It was both traumatic and distressing and the strain of almost three years of it was beginning to tell. The New Zealand trip itself was a wonderful wonderful adventure and although we were very sad when our elder daughter and family had emigrated there in 1992, it gave us this heaven sent opportunity to get far away and visit them for Christmas.

It is very hard to contemplate travelling this awe inspiring distance and especially flying at speeds of 600 miles an hour. Just try to relate this to a twenty seven hour flight and you begin to get it in perspective. It is a long, long way!

We had decided to travel down to Gatwick Airport by train and stay in that vicinity overnight. This was to give us the opportunity to visit an old cousin of my mother's whom we called Auntie May. She is amazing and at ninety years of age was just about as excited about this trip as we were, 'And just send me some postcards, it's supposed to be a wonderful country.' She was right but it was the people of New Zealand that impressed us the most. Shirley had commented on this, 'They are so very nice Mum and they don't moan all the time. They are smashing.'

Our journey was an experience in itself and although there is a stopover at Los Angeles, it is still a long and tedious flight. We flew via America with Air New Zealand and the attention and service from the cabin staff was first class. This is a great help especially on a flight of this duration. We landed finally at Auckland Airport in wonderful warm sunshine. We had left Scarborough on a typical wintery November day and landed in Summer!

It was so funny to see the Airport all beautifully decked out and decorated for Christmas. They had huge Christmas trees and Reindeers and sleighs everywhere but this was early summer wasn't it? What a mind boggling contrast. Going from Winter to Summer in two days is one thing but a Summer Christmas is just not on!

We were then to take an internal domestic flight to Rotorua where our Daughter lives. A bit like catching a bus really and it really did have a driver and conductor — well that's how it came across.

There were only about six of us on the plane and the pilot sat at the controls just in front of us. It was only a short flight but the one steward personally made us a cup of coffee and brought us magazines to read.

This was our introduction to the lovely people of New Zealand who ask you how you are before they ask you what you want.

We touched down at tiny Rotarua Airport — in a quite tiny plane.

Shirley, our son in law Rob and the children were there to meet us — they were watching from a small balcony. At first they didn't realise that it was our plane. They were expecting something much bigger. And then the waving, the smiling and the hugging. Yes it was Christmas and what a wonderful one at that. Our cares and worries were a million miles away.

CHAPTER SEVENTEEN
WRECKING RIGHTS AND TIMBERS

'Several wrecks of considerable value having at different times been drove ashore within the Royalty of Staintondale which doubtless were the property of those who were Lords of that Royalty', I quote from an account of all the charters, deeds and public records copied by request of the freeholders by one Lionel Charlton, a teacher of Mathematics at Whitby. The copies were made in 1776.

The account taken from Bundle 3 went on 'Great disputes and animosities arose in the days of Oliver Cromwell, which of the freeholders of that Manor were or were not the real Lords?'

It seemed proof of purchase lay with Christopher Beckwith and John Beswick but not before long and tedious legal action was pursued. The two freeholders I have mentioned made a deed of covenance of the Royalty to a William Bowes, William Worfolk, Henry Brough and James Harrison to hold in trust for all the other freeholders that 'hold land within the Manor of Staintondale'.

It was contested by a man called Gregory Hay. He considered himself the just Heir of all the Royalties and in the year 1655 for the sum of Eighty Pounds sold the Manor to his cousin William Hay who possessed a small tenement at the lower end of the Dale adjoining Hayburn Beck (spelt Heyburn). He was a tanner. The other freeholders considering themselves aggrieved filed a bill in Chancery against Gregory Hay and William Hay.

It was a fascinating case which I have read and re-read and Lionel Charlton seemed in doubt as to the truth even after the freeholders won the case. I have heard it said and very recently that a case is only as good as the last witness!

I would dearly love to pursue more of the legal complexities and contentious issued outlined over several centuries in these documents, but I have to conclude by saying that the calm tranquillity of this lovely dale belies a turbulent past.

I must quote just a few lines from this long account for the benefit of the legal minded.

'The freeholders made a reply to this answer and the two Hays rejoined to their reply, but all these things produced nothing. It was ordered by my Lord Chancellor that a number of interrogatories should be drawn up, a commission held and the deposition of witnesses taken on both sides, to make the truth of the matters now in dispute, more fully and plainly appear.' It goes on 'Proceedings went forward with great spirit on both sides.'

Ah well, somebody else has been down this road we tread, albeit in 1662 and I suspect the verdict then was possibly worth a 'back hander'. We now return to the present because I must relate some of this colourful past to our life at Eastside Farm and also to a previous owner.

The lovely old cow byre and the adjoining original stable which is now the Cafe and Shop was fully restored in 1988/89. It is a building rich in atmosphere and when we first came here I found it always to feel a cool and calm place. A haven of peace. Sometimes in the early evening when I do the rounds of locking up, I can just sit in this part that was the stable, and soak up the calmness of this special atmosphere. The Dawson family had lived here from 1931 and had kept a few cows as well as other livestock. Before the coming of electricity in the late fifties, oil lamps were used in both the house and buildings. In fact the lamp hooks are still evident inside the house.

On occasions when power cuts have been prolonged in winter time, we have had to resort to the use of an oil lamp. Its soft silent glow complemented by a log burning fire is a wonderful experience in itself.

In the farm buildings lamp holes were sometimes built into the walls and one such hole is provided in what is now the blacksmith's shop. We use it to house a loudspeaker for our P.A. system.

When the Dawsons lived here, one of the sister's jobs during the darker nights was to get the cows into the cow byre and have the oil lamp lit. Another sister who was a nurse I believe, went by train to work from Staintondale Station. It meant a walk across the fields every day along the route our visitors now walk for pleasure. When this particular sister arrived home it was her job to milk the cows.

When we bought the farm the cow byre was still functional. It had standings for four to five cows divided by original wooden partitions. In fact in the 1970s when self sufficiency was beginning to look like something of a necessity, we had a few dark brown Jersey cows which we hand milked and even made rich golden yellow butter.

When we first opened to the public in 1985, only this same cow byre was used as a tea room and small gift shop. It was quite funny really because we decided we would leave the raised standings and divisions in, to create a feature. This meant that because some of the tables were in this raised area, it meant a step up. Now everybody didn't see this step in spite of warning notices. It became a 'Two cups of tea please' and then after turning to sit down 'Oops! er would you mind filling the cups again please?'

I must explain that the counter ran the other way then, across the right hand gable end.

By 1988 the enterprise had developed sufficiently to necessitate some improvements. I applied to the Rural Development Commission for a grant to restore the small range of stone buildings we are talking about.

The roof was in a terrible state and the walls not much better. Sagging ridge stones showed that the walls were slowly being pushed outwards. Well this time luck was on our side and a small grant was made available to renovate this building and extend the cafe.

We started on November 18th 1988 and what a morning to choose. It had snowed overnight and the red clay pantiles were white over.

Undaunted, a young local chap Graham Steel and myself made a start. Two scaffold towers were erected and we commenced the laborious job of stripping off several hundred snow capped roof tiles.

'Just hope it doesn't snow again and stop the job', I said. I was also thinking what a time of year it was to be doing it, but we needed to be open for next summer. We progressed favourably, my assistant was an excellent worker.

After the tiles came the slate lats and lime plaster. What a filthy miserable job. The dirt and lime dust was everywhere. We were covered from head to toe.

Once this layer was removed the rafters were exposed and we had hoped that some might be saved. We were to be disappointed, they were all woodworm infested and rotten with damp and age. We decided the lot must go and also the pans (wall plates) as well. Off with the lot!

We were several days into this work by now, and believe it or not it had neither snowed nor rained. Now we had the square of the building to examine — the walls. At this point I had a minor brain-wave. We could stabilise these old walls by pouring a mixture of wettish sharp sand and cement down the cavities. This was quite quickly accomplished and we could get straight on with the new roof structure.

It was important to retain the original principles and pegged purlins. You don't talk about sympathetic restoration and use what are known as wood engineering and purpose made trusses. I shall not go on with a detailed account of all this work. The finished product is there to be seen and one I am proud of.

What is of interest is the level of the cafe extension floor. It now runs about two thirds of the way up the original stable doorway that you see from the outside. That was the difference in floor levels. And suffice to say that the old stable originally had a loft. The loft level was the beam end you see sawn off and a small wood spoked wheel mounted on it.

At least it gave us a hole to fill with all the debris taken from the roof and stone from the hole we cut through the wall. The breaking through bit, another Des masterpiece but that's another story. We got the whole lot finished and flagged by January 26th 1989, Ann's birthday. And without her knowing, planned and presented her with a surprise birthday party inside this very building.

The chapter is called Wrecking Rights and Timber. Well I have to mention here that for centuries along this coast, not only did the wrecks give up their lucrative cargo, they also provided superb timber of oak and pitch pine for the building and repair of these farms and outbuildings. We have some wonderful stout oak beams in the roof of our house. Timber so hard you cannot easily drive a nail in. There is evidence of these timbers in all our buildings but one piece in particular is a feature in the shop.

It is a sailing ship beam from the stem of the vessel and the draught marks are in Roman numerals. Possibly sixteenth century, who knows? Anyway there it is and it forms one of the main principles in the centre of the back half of the roof.

So there you have it. The stone for the building came from local stone quarries and not least the cliffs. The timber was provided by the graveyard of wooden hulled sailing ships wrecked along the coast. And the money? Well take your pick. We have heard of the wrecking rights and the considerable value of these vessels. We have heard of the smuggling and the consequences of that. We have not heard too much about farming but we have heard some of these people described in court as the Gentlemen farmers of Staintondale, and the riding to hounds.

With apologies to Rudyard Kipling a line from his 'Smugglers Song' 'And watch the wall, my darling, while the gentlemen go by!'

CHAPTER EIGHTEEN
BOMBED OUT OF COURT

We were up early on the morning of the trial, in fact we booked an alarm call with British Telecom. Something that seemed ridiculous at the time but today we had a train to catch. Ann had discovered that trains into Hull ran from Driffield on a regular basis. It would save the hassle of facing a lot of traffic in Hull and also avoid having to worry about parking. We had been told to arrive early at the Court so that we could meet our Barrister and be briefed on procedure. The case had been set down for trial at Kingston upon Hull County Court for March 22nd, 23rd and 24th 1994. Today was the first day.

We drove along our new farm road to the point where we had to stop and Ann opened the gate. I drove slowly through on to what was in fact the disputed area and waited for her to get back in the car.

Consciously I looked towards our neighbours' cottage 'Were they as worried and concerned as I was?' My thoughts led me to looking over the access we had created and I thought how tidy and attractive it looked. Soon the daffodils would be blooming and the new trees bursting their buds.

I resolved it was worth fighting for. This access and the lovely new road to the farm with its wide verges and trees was a dream come true. We had battled with prejudice and unreasonable atti-tudes for years. This was my road.

We set off for Driffield and talked about anything but the trial. I was trying to appear nonchalant and unruffled but Ann looked ill. She was as white as a ghost and under a great deal of stress. And it showed. Underneath my assumed blandness I was working hard to keep my head. Something I fervently believe in.

Looking back over the last three years I think I was wondering whether for Ann's sake I should have tried to settle. She is not equipped to handle arguments or disagreement and I knew she was having a hard time. We had convinced ourselves that win or lose it was only money but if someone's health is at stake it is a very different ball game. Anyway too late now, let us hope that justice would be done and we could get on with the rest of our lives.

I think it was my own Father who told me that you could hang for your principles. It looked like I was going to lay mine on the line.

We arrived at Driffield well ahead of schedule and sat in the car going through the morning mail. Some very good news amongst it from Yorkshire and Humberside Tourist Board Tourism Advisory Service. It was for some proposed budget accommodation here at the farm. I have got to say that it was very favourable and this really pleased me.

The deserted platform at Driffield Station was quite a shock. My memories were of bustling platforms and busy porters. Today it was a pay train — a one man band. Never mind it is still rather special travelling by train. Something quite reassuring and relaxing.

We arrived in Hull and took a taxi to the Courthouse. Our destiny and possibly the destiny of the farm would be at stake over the next three days. We really were facing triumph or disaster and the legal process is slow moving.

The staff at this impressive Court building were very pleasant. They were efficient, courteous and helpful and we soon found ourselves in this modern complex having a cup of coffee. It was all very civilised. Soon our solicitor arrived who duly introduced us to our Counsel. He too was very nice — and, er, very young I thought inwardly. Or was it me coming to grips with my age. Prior to this I had a word with my old adversary who had been the area surveyor at the time of the planning dispute. He was there as an expert witness together with his assistant whom I had also previously dealt with. Expert was the word, his evidence was a masterstroke as we shall hear later. We were just about to be ushered into court when there was a rather large hiccup. Quite amazing and quite unprecedented I would imagine. Well for the particular reasons you are going to read.

It seemed that the judge selected to hear the case had already heard about us and the Shire Horse Farm. Apparently his wife and her Mother had visited the farm and gone home so impressed they had talked about nothing else.

This particular judge having listened to all this, felt that he could not conduct or give judgment in the trial with total impartiality. He felt that his personal knowledge would make this difficult. For this reason he had elected to stand down and another judge had to be summoned. That put an end to the start of the morning's proceedings. The trial would now start at 2.30 p.m.

Our two friends and previous neighbours had now arrived and a wonderful light-hearted exchange of greetings relieved the pressure. They were our sunshine that day. We decided that we would see the sights of Hull and then have lunch together.

At 2.20 p.m. we returned to the Court and were duly seated in the awesome surroundings of the Court room. A bit like a church really. Well this was a day of judgment. The first day of the trial is the opportunity of the Plaintiffs to give clear and compelling evidence to show good reason for their grievance. They have to try and convince the judge of their assumed legal rights and claims. Four witnesses were called, one of the plaintiff's being the chief witness on their side.

One question was put to both the plaintiff and his brother. I could not understand the significance of this question, nor of the response it brought. Was it properly understood? They were asked who had negotiated the sale and was it through an agent. Both said through their agent. The plain truth of the matter was that I was approached by the plaintiff's brother one day whilst cutting grass in one of our fields. He asked me why I had shown no interest in a block of land adjoining my property which they had put on the open market. I replied that I was not prepared to enter blind negotiations by bidding against something that had no ceiling. Matching one bid against another in other words, and knowing because our water supply sprung from this very block of land I had to secure it.

It was a gamble I had taken but it had worked. Against this background I agreed that I would talk to their agent with a view to establishing a fair value. It was then agreed that I should meet the two brothers personally and jointly and agree an acceptable price that we could shake hands on. It was a private meeting and it took place in the yard on their property. From this meeting and subsequent agreement the sale of the land was duly completed. This land had other attractive benefits, it would give us the opportunity to create a private farm road sometime in the future. For almost twenty years we had struggled with the problems of an access road not on our property but for many years solely maintained by ourselves. It had caused aggravation, confrontation and animosity.

I was previous in my assumption here and you are now reading about what it did bring. Even more aggravation, confrontation and animosity.

The two main witnesses were in turn cross examined by our Counsel. His manner with them was to say the least, charming and even at times beguiling. They said everything he wanted to hear them say.

"Oh yes we fenced the field from the road. Well folk kept leaving the gate open. Oh yes I can remember the road at the time it was rough and they were driving on the field. Well the fence stopped all that, they had to stick to the road. Well yes we left a bit of room for combines and things, they would have damaged the fence."

Our Counsel was purring.

"Well of course you did, you didn't want to be rounding up straying cattle. Of course you wouldn't want people driving on your grass pasture — you made them stick to the road. Naturally you left some space at the side. You didn't want your fence damaged did you? Of course not."

They fell willingly and eagerly as Counsel smiled back at them. Now he said 'Does the name F. Bloggs mean anything to you?' 'Oh yes he was our grandad', came the reply. 'Parish Councillor I believe?' 'Oh yes, that's the same man', confirmed the witness. I wonder if you can help me here? I have a document which was part of the survey carried out by the Parish Council in 1951. It was conducted by North Yorkshire County Council'. Our Counsel went on, 'It was with regard to several roads in the area and included the road in question. With regard to this particular road the question was, 'Is this road a public highway maintainable at public expense?' The answer given is yes and the document is signed F. Bloggs — would that be the same man?' Counsel paused. If gloating was within this man's make up it didn't show. He just kept smiling. 'Well yes that would be him!'

In a T.V. drama it would be followed with 'I rest my case'. This was real life drama and I wanted to applaud. I heard Counsel tell our solicitor afterwards that they would never have a better day and I was in full support of that statement. Together with our two friends and our legal representatives we were in high spirits. Gleeful would be a good word. I was feeling grateful as well because I realised a lot of hard work had gone into the preparation of our defence. Not

I wonder if you can help me here . . . ?

least the former Area Surveyor and I referred to his masterstroke earlier — it was the signed document. Our Counsel had earned my admiration too. His presentation was first class.

Day two dawned and found us in good spirits. Ann's colour had returned to near normal and today on our journey we openly discussed the merits of the case. In the event it turned out to be both an ordeal and a cliff-hanger and not quite what we thought.

It was now our turn to give evidence and our Counsel had held conference and explained what the procedure would be. Looking at me he said 'And you — you must not stray from the issue. The issue is the status of the road and not the rights or wrongs of this action. Keep your answers short and as brief as possible.' He obviously knew my limitations but I was also very aware also of my inclination to get carried away by my own personal viewpoint. The reason perhaps why I write these books.

At last I took the witness stand and found myself taking the oath. Their Counsel started questioning by showing a series of photographs. They clearly showed some parts of the road no longer in regular use but they were not areas I was conversant with. This caused me some concern because I found questions on these difficult to answer.

He eventually got to the point of the new access and I think he was confused by the original requirement of County Council and the compromise made because of some difficulty over land not in our possession. He seemed to be implying that I had not properly carried out the planning conditions imposed. He also seemed to be suggesting that I had not informed the plaintiffs of my intended new access.

I was getting very confused and felt that I was making a mess of something I should have found easy. When he again pursued the question of not fully implementing the conditions and widening the road for the length specified, I was choked.

The length required had included a sign belonging to our neighbours who at the time of the site meeting, I still regarded as friends. It would have meant removing this sign and the grass area it stood on and surfacing that piece as well. I had made the point about this friendship to the surveyor and asked, 'Can't I just skirt round that bit?'

Now they were accusing me of opting out of my responsibilities as well as taking this distressing legal action against us. It was just too much I just broke down. They were our friends . . .

After a short time the questioning continued. 'It was not very neighbourly of you not to inform my clients of your intentions now was it?'

Well here again I should have jumped in with both feet and said 'Well it wasn't very neighbourly of them to sell us this land knowing why we wanted it and then taking legal action to try and stop us using it!' He also said that we had received the summons before the planning approval certificate which was not the case.

I wanted to argue and I wanted to explode. This wasn't the situation at all and I felt frustrated. Twice I had gone round to these neighbours and twice I had written and made overtures to try and end the dispute. Now it seemed I was being accused of hostility and it hurt. Well bearing in mind my Barrister's briefing and with Kipling still my mentor I decided that the bit that says 'And yet not look too good nor talk too wise' had to be me that morning. The case continued and our friend and previous neighbour took the stand. His evidence was clear and forthright. He knew the road to be a public highway and he had purchased his farm on that basis. He was in no doubt and he still had records to prove it.

North Yorkshire County Council witness was excellent. Indeed both the former Area Surveyor and his assistant were very effective. The witness in the senior position produced evidence and reference from 1929 onwards and maps from long before. His *coup de grace* came in the shape of the document I have previously described, and an attempt by opposition Counsel to discount it, was met with blow for blow moves a master chess player would relish. I should think he left the court in no doubt. Then followed the submission by our Counsel and he was very professional in this also. He cited a case Minton v Ramage and took it through to conclusion. It sounded a watertight and comparable submission. He left the opposition with the burden of proof. Their barrister then stood up and began speaking, he seemed to cite every case in the book that might or might not be relevant. Was this a confusion tactic or was this really such a unique and questionable situation? I was beginning to wonder myself.

His closing remarks left me feeling angry and disillusioned. 'My clients are looking for something fairly substantial in the way of damages. This land is off course a valuable piece of land'.

He was talking about the 7sq metres or thereabouts that had once formed part of the verge and were now part of the road.

'When I say value' he went on 'I am not talking about a price relative to the value of the land but the value relative to this successful commercial development. It could be described as a ransom strip!'

I was livid. Yes that summed it up, we were being held to ransom and were in a situation which I had referred to in correspondence with my solicitor as blackmail. That is why I was in court today. I had refused to pay. The judge then came to his summing up and said that he would proceed without delay and give judgment. What a relief. The nightmare was to end one way or another. He slowly and deliberately went through the background to the dispute and outlined the evidence given on both sides. Then he thanked those who had given such clear and conclusive evidence. It was all very correct and formal with no hint of partiality. I would describe his manner as inscrutable and as it should be.

Well that was fine but sitting waiting and anticipating was like being in death row. What was the verdict, which way would the pendulum swing? We got our answer and my eyes filled up. I looked at Ann and I think we could have stood up and cheered. Yes it was a highway, and the claims made by North Yorkshire County Council were proven and beyond doubt. He went on 'And now we came to the question of the verge. Is it or is it not part of that highway?'

This was the all important part of his judgment. It was crucial because if it was not, then our access was effectively a no access. It was a very stressful and nailbiting situation and my heart was pounding. This pounding has continued on and off ever since the trial. He started on his summary, we sat tense and forward on our seats. Just at that terminal point a man appeared behind the witness box and to the left of the bench. He was both apologetic and earnest and looked embarrassed. 'Did you not hear the audio alarm? Clear the court quickly there has been a bomb alert!' We didn't wait to be told twice and the next few minutes found us in the shelter of the building next door — it was a church.

Was I dreaming all this? I felt like pinching myself. My assistant had joked with me about an article we had read in the National press about a man in Germany who had taken a bomb and a gun to court. He had shot the judge and then blown the court up including himself.

I in reply had said that if I blew the court up it would be with me on the outside. She had laughed and said 'Well just don't go taking any bombs.' I just could not believe it.

We stood there in the cold, it was mid to late afternoon and only the second but what was to be, the final day. Our destiny hung in the balance. What a time to happen and what a catastrophe if we had to come again tomorrow. There would be no sleep to-night. Our legal repre-sentatives also seemed to be look-ing a little less con-fident. They thought we should win and anyway the road was proven. . . . of course if the verge isn't part of it, it is going to cost you a lot of money.

This was the worst possible few minutes of my life. The talk was 'Had the Judge gone home and if not would he carry on with his judgment at this late hour?'

Relief was at hand. An usher appeared and said we could return to the Court-house, the area had been checked and our case was to be concluded.

We filed back into the Courtroom and took up our positions. The opposition on the left hand side and us on the right. Again the judge started to deliberate and I was shaking. This time I couldn't altogether follow the drift of his comments and I found this a bit disturbing. In front of me I had a clipboard and paper and I was doodling just to occupy my mind. A thought about luck came into my head and I was then remembering a telephone conversation only days earlier with a friend who had really experienced some rotten luck. He had been to the farm last year and asked me for a horseshoe. This recent telephone call had been to tell me how much his luck had changed since he got the horseshoe. A new job, a new baby, and good prospects. He said he now had three of them nailed to various doors.

With this in mind I started to sketch three horseshoes on the pad and elaborate them with shadings and nailholes. Just as I had finished came the verdict.

'And in conclusion and in view of the evidence put forward by both plaintiffs and other witnesses I have to find in favour of the defendants. The verge in this instance is part of the public highway.'

We were exuberant. The relief was almost too much to bear and everybody on our side was smiling. We had won!

As soon as the Judge retired it was hand shakes all round. This had not been easy for anybody and a great deal of work, thought and effort had gone into our defence.

Before the proceedings had quite ended our Counsel had responded to the Judge's verdict. He then said that the cost of this case to his clients had been considerable — well into five figures. On the other side, the cost to the plaintiff had been nil. Could he therefore ask leave of court under section 18 Legal Aid Act 1988 to seek to recover some of these costs out of the legal aid fund and directions given for further conduct of the case.

I shall not get into technical details here in case I am wrong but it seemed we may be in a position to claim help from the public purse. The Judge granted this request and then turning to the opposition he stated. 'And even had I found in favour of the plaintiffs the award for damages would have been small, no more than three hundred pounds!' If that wasn't a rebuff then I misunderstood the point he was making. A bomb scare had driven us out of court and now it seemed the opposition were being bombed out!

I must end this my third book with a comment I made some years ago when I could see a dispute developing. Take heed 'There is no such thing as victory when neighbours can no longer live in harmony!'

One previous neighbour who I have mentioned in my second book always refers to the old adage, 'Live and let live' and it is sound advice. There are some wonderful people in the world and we meet a lot of them here at the farm. Keep coming to see us and keep reading. One day I shall write about my peaceable, uneventful and tranquil life.

Appendix I

This is a copy of the letter which I sent to every member of the committee, together with extracts from the survey of a thousand visitors to the Farm.

October 1990

Dear County Councillor,

In the event of my small rural enterprise coming before the North York Moors Planning Committee again, I offer the following observations.

Without this diversification, my small 50 acre farm is totally unviable. I have worked long and hard for fifteen years to create what many believe to be the best small rural attraction in the NYMNP. Our recent survey of over 1000 visitors here confirms this (samples enclosed). The survey also shows quite clearly that neither access problems or passing difficulties were encountered. I am asking for nothing more than fair play. Not favours, not financial support, just fair play. There are seven farms served by Downdale Road, an agricultural and marine engineering shop, a caravan site, plus other domestic and holiday cottages.

Highways are asking for four passing places constructed to their specifications, all at my expense. I did not learn of this until after the meeting in January, when these conditions were imposed. In fact, the detailed agreement and plan did not arrive until June. It added up to a staggering commitment approaching £20,000, including a bond amount of £4,600!

I have offered to bear the cost of two passing places as a gesture of goodwill in line with the degree of my responsibility, and I have written to Mr A Burns explaining my position. In addition to this of course, there is my offer of the provision of a new farm road, which incidentally I have now implemented at a cost of around £4000. We are only a small seasonal enterprise. I have no wish to go bankrupt along with a lot of other small businesses now struggling. More than that, seven seasonal jobs go with me.

I sincerely hope County Councillors will share my anxiety and not withdraw support.

Yours sincerely, Tony Jenkins

Appendix II

Specimen comments on Traffic Survey form:

An entertaining and informative afternoon. Well worth encouraging especially one with so little impact on the environment.

•••

We have visited Staintondale Shire Horse Farm for the last four years (including 1990) sometimes twice in one holiday. From memory we have never encountered any other traffic on the road to and from the farm. Only those who are really interested visit the farm, many people making return visits. It should be retained in its present form.

•••

'Rural' nature of access road is part of the charm and realism of the place. Definitely worthwhile — awful shame if people (especially young people and children) didn't have the opportunity to see these traditional things. This is my second visit — and equally as enjoyable as my first. Access has been no problem. We are staying on a farm which uses the same access and there have been no problems in the entire week. Numbers visiting in the peak of the holiday season appear to be relatively small and therefore traffic problems are unlikely to be created. This is especially so, as the centre operates on a 'timetable' basis and therefore traffic is likely to be travelling in the same direction at any given time. As an ex Police Officer I found no difficulty, no traffic hazard and no congestion whilst approaching this worthwhile enterprise.

•••

We think everything here is just right. Natural and beautiful. We found no difficulty at all getting down here. Extremely enjoyable.

•••

Well worth the journey — you expect winding roads in the countryside and drive accordingly. Half of its charm is the delightful ride to get here!! — keep up the good work!! This is our 5th visit, enjoyed it every time. Never encountered any difficulties entering or leaving on the narrow road. We find this is one of the many attractions Staintondale holds. We will come again and again. Think again before proposing making changes that could be environmentally damaging to the current showpiece that is evidently attractive to all who visit.

•••

The rural charm could easily be spoilt by too much planning! Don't change the country lane at all. Its quiet, pleasant and very welcoming the way it is. After all it's supposed to be a working farm lane not a speed track.

•••

Visitors will realize that local roads to a farm will be narrow and therefore take more care than usual. It is this type of enterprise that I have visited the Park to see. I have been down many other minor roads with as little difficulty during the course of my holiday here. I find it incredible that a Planning Authority should not wish to encourage this type of enterprise in the Park. An extremely interesting piece of 'Old England' that should be helped and encouraged. The quietness and serenity is most calming in hectic living of today.

•••

Staintondale Shire Horse Farm
June 1990.

If

If you can keep your head when all about you
    Are losing theirs and blaming it on you,
If you can trust yourself when all men doubt you,
    But make allowance for their doubting too;
If you can wait and not be tired of waiting,
    Or being lied about, don't deal in lies,
Or being hated don't give way to hating,
    And yet don't look too good, nor talk too wise:

If you can dream — and not make dreams your master;
    If you can think — and not make thoughts your aim:
If you can meet with Triumph and Disaster
    And treat those two impostors just the same:
If you can bear to hear the truth you've spoken
    Twisted by knaves to make a trap for fools,
Or watch the things you gave your life to, broken,
And stoop and build 'em up with worn-out tools:

If you can make one heap of all your winnings
    And risk it on one turn of pitch-and-toss,
And lose, and start again at your beginnings
    And never breathe a word about your loss;
If you can force your heart and nerve and sinew
    To serve your turn long after they are gone,
And so hold on when there is nothing in you
    Except the Will which says to them: 'Hold on!'

If you can talk with crowds and keep your virtue,
    Or walk with Kings — nor lose the common touch,
If neither foes nor loving friends can hurt you,
    If all men count with you, but none too much;
If you can fill the unforgiving minute
    With sixty seconds' worth of distance run,
Yours is the Earth and everything that's in it,
    And — which is more — you'll be a Man, my son!

Rudyard Kipling